THE
UNINVITED
PASSENGER

Copyright © 2025 by Isabella Tousignant

REL Print Group,
a Hezzie Mae Publication
Duluth, MN.
www.HezzieMae.com

All rights reserved. Hezzie Mae supports copyright. Copyright fuels creativity, encourages diverse voices, promotes free speech, and creates a vibrant culture. Thank you for complying with copyright laws by not reproducing, scanning, or distributing any part of this book in any form without permission from the publisher.

ISBN: 979-8-9997402-1-2

Cover Design: Chani Becker @chanibecker.com

THE UNINVITED
PASSENGER

Isabella Tousignant

Duluth, MN

Dedication

To Trish, my loving wife, best friend, and true love. I could not have done this and would not be who I am today without your love and support. You are the one constant light in my life. You have been by my side through thick and thin, and your love has never failed.

In Memorial

Louis and Isabel Tousignant, my father and mother.
Your personal sacrifice and dedication to your eight children are the reasons for all of our individual success as human beings. You led us by examples of honesty, faith, compassion, and respect for others. I'm not always able, but I try my best to apply these acts of selflessness and courage each day of my life.

Foreword

·

As long as I have traveled through this life, an uninvited passenger has accompanied me. An obnoxious backseat driver, issuing directions I refused to follow. I could distract myself from this annoying pest, but never completely escaped the insistent demand to take an alternate route.

New cities, new careers, and new friends did not make any difference. These were interim diversions in my effort to evade the inevitable conclusion that I would need to acknowledge. I was sixty-three years old before accepting that the passenger was in reality my true self, crying out for help.

I have struggled with gender dysphoria for six complete decades. I think I have enough lived experience to understand what it is and what it is not. It is very real and incessant. Emotional distress, psychological despair, self-doubt, self-loathing, and a constant battle for acceptance are just a few of the challenges.

Three-quarters of a century involving extensive medical, scientific, and therapeutic research has resulted in effective treatments, allowing transgender individuals to live full and productive lives. Strict evidence-based guidelines are followed in diagnosis and care management. I owe my well-being to the dedicated professionals who have improved my life beyond any expectations.

Perhaps I can better explain what gender dysphoria is not. It is not an ideology. That definition has been thrown around a lot lately, as if a conspiracy exists to undermine the traditional definition of male and female, starting a war against Christianity and defying the laws of creation. I must have missed that meeting. As a matter of fact, no such groupthink exists.

However, if you want to gain and keep power, there is no better method than inventing an enemy, declaring yourself the guardian and protector of women and children, and then vowing to destroy this manufactured enemy.

First, you introduce the lie. Next, you spread it in various versions, and your accomplices spread similar lies to propagate and reinforce the misinformation. This is a proven method of distributing manure and raising significant stench.

When people hear something frequently that aligns with their values, they often perceive it as the truth. After all, it's the validation they were longing for.

There are so many examples to select, but this particular one struck hard because it was not only false, but completely ridiculous and outside the orbit of possibility.

Donald Trump at a campaign rally in Wisconsin just before the November 2024 Presidential election: "Can you imagine you're a parent and your son leaves the house and you say, 'Jimmie, I love you so much. Go have a good day in school' and your son comes back with a brutal operation." He added, "Can you even imagine this? What the hell is wrong with our country?"

He addressed the Moms for Liberty group a few days later with similar nonsense, saying, "The transgender thing is incredible. Think of it. Your kid goes to school and comes home a few days later with an operation. The school decides what is going to happen to your child."

There is too much to unpack here. First, the crowd reaction was loud booing, followed by cheering their hero for saying he would fix that. I assume they all believed every word by their response. Secondly, schools must have changed significantly! All my school nurse had was a thermometer, a box of Band-Aids, and a nap bed. Are we to believe there is a surgery center with doctors capable of miraculously changing little Jimmie into a girl and sending him home the same day, or doing this in any timeframe at all?

No evidence exists of any such event or even as much as a suggestion of such a preposterous undertaking. In fact, in the states where gender-affirming surgery is legal for minors, parental consent is absolutely required, and surgery rarely occurs. These are false and damaging claims.

I have the utmost respect for teachers — their commitment to their students, their sacrifice of high-paying careers, and the scorn they face from parents. And yet, they are the first to spend their own money on school supplies that are not budgeted. However, the falsehoods persist, and those spreading them remain indifferent to their impact.

Another drum beaten daily is the insulting concept of a "woke culture virus," accusing transgender adults of spreading their "disease" to your children, indoctrinating them into their way of life, and convincing them to change genders.

Only someone capable of inflicting horror on another human being could come up with a scenario this diabolical and reprehensible. I have suffered from gender dysphoria all of my life, and I would not wish this on the children of my worst enemy. Do they believe that if someone is born blind, that person would kidnap children and take away their sight? They would say that if it increased their political influence, as nothing else matters to them.

Furthermore, being "anti-woke" is the hill Republicans have chosen to die on. So much of their success can be attributed to this slanderous, racist assault on black culture in America. The expression "woke" gained momentum in the 2010s, meaning one should be politically and socially aware of injustice, primarily in the African American community, and is commonly associated with the Black Lives Matter movement. It has nothing to do with the culture wars being bundled into "wokeness."

The terms *wokeism* and *woke virus* have been repeatedly cried out in derogatory ways and have obstructed the civil rights of various marginalized groups in America. It has proven to be the bigots' most effective weapon. If you don't like a group of people, claim they are "woke," and magically, they become an enemy of the self-righteous.

Do I believe all Republican politicians are racist? No, but those who tolerate and support these tactics have to look into their own hearts.

Then, there's the issue of transgender people in sports: another serious subject that has been lied about to boost political ratings. Campaign ads falsely showing a seven-foot-tall man in a bad wig towering over a frightened small girl on a basketball court are incredibly offensive. It only gets worse when the voice-over says, "We need to keep men out of girls' sports," rather than, "We need to keep trans girls out of girls' sports." The image and wording are blatantly false and inflammatory. Who would want this to happen to anyone? It never has.

Is this a subject that requires discussion? Absolutely. A reasonable solution can be found if we bother to look for one.

But it won't be discussed because, again, there's too much power at stake to let go of a controversy you have been demagoguing.

A few pertinent facts: there are 520,000 athletes in the NCAA — 293,000 male and 229,000 female. Reportedly, fewer than 10 are transgender. That's hardly an epidemic or a takeover.

Every time I turn on my television, I hear certain congresswomen harping about the "takeover of women's sports by men pretending to be women." It's like a knife going through my heart, because I know this is the furthest possible statement from the truth. Somewhere in America, people are getting angrier by the minute at the god-awful transgender people who are ruining women's sports, convincing our children they are not who they think they are, invading women's restrooms, and molesting them (also not true). They hear this often enough that it becomes a reality to them.

Sarah McBride, the first trans woman elected to the U.S. Congress, was attacked by congresswomen who not only pressured House Speaker Johnson to bar her from using women's restrooms in the Capitol but also staged a false scenario to entrap her.

Directly after the rule went into effect, one of them actually screamed, "There's a man in the ladies' room!" in an attempt to set Congresswoman McBride up. It was not her in the restroom. I feel bad for the poor cis woman who was in there. She must've been terribly embarrassed when she came out alone to find them waiting.

What kind of rotting heart must you have to do this to someone? Is there no better way to spend the taxpayers' dollars? Wasting your time and our money trying to incriminate your fellow members of Congress?

Like many transgender people, I am a productive member of society and have been for many years. I have met doctors, lawyers, business owners, and other dedicated transgender people in all walks of life who work hard, pay their taxes, and expect more of their government than what we are now seeing.

Violence against transgender people is skyrocketing. I read about another attack or murder daily. If you think lies have no consequences, you need to open your eyes. False, hateful rhetoric gives permission to those who are looking to justify their acts of anger.

Why is all of this important in telling my story? Because it is what my story has become. I spent four years searching through my past, reliving agonizing moments, and pouring my heart onto the pages. Shortly after completion, the world around me darkened.

All of my hopefulness and visions of living as my true self in a place where I could experience acceptance, enjoying the last years of my life in peace and feelings of congruence, are now under siege.

The identity I had worked so hard to come to terms with and finally brought into the daylight was being erased each day with a new executive order designed to make me invisible again. But I see myself clearly, and you cannot blind me.

The passenger is now the driver and will never take a back seat to anyone again.

Chapter One:
With Me from the Start

It was mid-afternoon. I didn't have a costume yet. We were in a rush to find something for that night. I was excited as Mom and I walked to the neighborhood variety store to see what we could scrounge up. Kids were playing in their yards, chasing each other around, energy high in anticipation of the fun to come. Passing a mother and her young daughter on the sidewalk, my eyes fixed on the little girl. She was wearing a gypsy girl costume.

"So what do you want to be this year?" Mom asked.

I didn't have to think about it. I pointed back at the girl. "That's what I want to be."

"Are you sure? That's a girl's costume. Don't you want to be a cowboy or something else?"

I was very certain with my answer: "Yeah, Mom, I'm sure."

"Well then, let's see if there's something we can put together for you."

The Uninvited Passenger

I felt stirred up in a way I recognized. I had only a few years of memories, but this was a familiar desire.

Last year, one of my older brother's Boy Scout troops put on a production of *Snow White*. They thought it would be funny to have me play one of the seven dwarves, so I got to watch the boy selected to play Snow White. During dress rehearsal, I was fascinated by his transformation from boring kid to princess. I wanted that transformation for myself.

The prior year, the year my oldest sister had gotten married, I was a dapper little ring bearer in my white tuxedo jacket and black trousers. My sisters all thought it was cute that I followed the flower girl everywhere at the reception, thinking I had a crush on her. I remember it differently: I loved her lacy pink dress and wanted it for myself.

Now, Mom and I were on our way to pick out my own dress. I was ecstatic. In the store, Mom reached for a scarf and wrapped it around my head for a fit. She picked out some beads and a sash for my waist.

"Now all we need is to find you a long skirt and a peasant blouse."

Back home, Mom pinned a skirt around me and found an off-the-shoulder blouse that worked. Completing the outfit with the beads and sash, she combed my hair forward and tied the scarf around my head. She added rosy cheeks and red lips. I was ready.

"Look at you! You *are* a gypsy girl now."

Seeing myself as a girl for the first time was like nothing I had ever known. A warm, glowing feeling filled my heart. I felt perfect: this was how I was meant to feel.

I was still too young to go along with my older brothers, so Mom took me trick-or-treating. The full moon shone down like honey. The warm autumn air flowed around my skirt. With Mom holding my hand, I bounded through the neighborhood. At each stop, my wonderful feelings magnified as people complimented Mom on how cute her 'daughter' was. Being referred to as a girl and thought of as my mother's daughter was the most wonderful thing I could imagine. I wanted this night to last forever.

Returning home, I raised my candy bag above my head and dumped its contents on the living room floor. I sat on the floor, taking my time to assess the night's bounty. I was also stalling so I could continue being a girl.

"C'mon, let's get you ready for bed," Mom said.

"Can't I keep my costume on, Mom?"

"Just a little longer, but then it's off to bed."

Taking off my costume, I felt like a girl in a fairy tale stripped of her magical powers. As Mom tucked me into bed and turned off the light, I felt an emptiness I did not like or understand.

I stayed in bed longer than usual the next morning, enjoying the lingering bliss from my enchanted night. I felt such a strong sense of self as a girl and a certainty that I did not want to leave her behind.

For the first time, I realized that this was not just a passing whim, but something deeper, something that I couldn't explain to myself or anyone else. Puzzled, I decided to keep this to myself for the time being. What happened next strengthened that decision and drove my identity further inward.

Bouncing down the staircase, I turned the corner and noticed a close friend of my oldest brother sitting in our living room. Two of my brothers, the ones just a few years older than me, were lying on the floor with their heads propped up on their elbows, watching Saturday morning cartoons.

"Look, you guys," the friend said in a taunting voice, "Your little sister is finally out of bed. Was she getting her beauty rest, or was she just having trouble with her makeup?"

Obviously, he was aware of my Halloween costume.

"I know, let's take you to JCPenney and find you some cute little dresses, so you can dress like a girl all the time. I'll bet you'd like that, wouldn't you, sweetie pie?"

In my heart, I would have loved that, but I was old enough to know when I was being attacked. The older of my brothers rolled over off his elbows and lifted his head.

"Leave him alone, he's six years old. Give him a break already, will you?"

"Okay, fine. If you want your little brother to grow up as a sissy, I'll leave it alone. I'm just trying to teach him a lesson."

I admired my brothers, and I was angry that he had humiliated me in front of them.

"Yeah, just shut up," I said with all the courage I could muster.

"Oh, you're just so cute when you're angry," he shot back.

Upset, I started towards the front door.

He got out of his chair and ran after me. He grabbed my forearm and twisted me around, feigning sympathy.

"C'mon, get back here! I was only joking with you. Can't you handle a little teasing? It's all in good fun."

Teasing, I could handle, but this touched a nerve. The cloud I had been floating on dissipated, leaving me without the innocent joy I felt just a short time ago. It wasn't good fun. I was being shamed, and I knew it.

Pulling my arm back, I ran out the front door into the yard.

Sitting on the front stoop by myself, I couldn't understand why he embarrassed me in front of my brothers. Why would something so harmless, something I loved so much, be such a problem for him? Did other grown-ups think this way, too? I didn't want to find out. I wasn't about to let anyone make me feel like that again.

I resolved to find ways to disguise my feelings. I would act like my brothers. After all, they were boys. All I had to do was mimic their behaviors, or even exaggerate them. I would work hard to develop a tough image. A fierce competitor who excelled in sports. No one could ever doubt that I was anything other than 'all boy.'

Privately, I dreamed of being a girl and relived that Halloween repeatedly. I clung to those memories and imagined worlds where I could exist as a girl and not be ashamed. This was the beginning of my contradiction: a denial that was never accepted from within, causing lifelong turmoil.

It would be a long time before I had the opportunity to express myself outwardly again. Hiding my feelings became a way of life. It wasn't until I was almost twelve years old that I risked being embarrassed again. It became one of the fondest memories I have of my mom.

I knew this would be the last Halloween before I was too old to go trick-or-treating in costume. I was desperate to dress up as a girl for my costume, but I couldn't let anyone know it. I thought that the only way I could make this work would be if Mom suggested it, so I'd have to be clever. Upstairs, I rummaged through drawers and slammed them so she could hear me. I stomped on the floor, going from room to room to make it noticeable. I continued down the stairs, then paced around the room where she was sitting.

"Settle down! Haven't you found a costume yet? It's going to be dark soon, so you'd better make up your mind," she said.

"I can't find anything. This is going to be my last time before I'm too old, and I want something special."

Mom thought for a moment, turned, and looked up from the program she was watching.

"Why don't you dress up as a girl? You love doing that, and besides, you look so cute."

I was surprised that she actually suggested what I wanted, and a little stunned that she knew how much I enjoyed it. I hesitated, masking my excitement.

"Sure, I guess that would be okay," I replied.

Okay? I was overjoyed. Mom's acknowledgment of my love for being a girl and her saying I was cute was a tender moment for me. I imagined that I really was her daughter, and we had just shared something special that would remain our secret.

She helped me put together an outfit. We went all-out this time: red fingernails and lipstick, her wig, a pleated skirt, and a soft sweater. I was in heaven again.

Gender dysphoria hadn't been publicly defined at that time, or even mentioned.

Yet, somehow, Mom was in tune with my feelings. Clinical definition or not, she knew what was in my heart and loved me unconditionally.

Others around me had a different reaction. Back in school the next day, the teasing started during morning recess. Some of my classmates had seen me the night before, and I became a source of their amusement. I still had some nail polish on that I couldn't completely remove. One of the boys pointed that out to everyone within earshot. He was a known bully, and I anticipated trouble. He purposely ran into me and knocked me to the ground. I stood up and dusted myself off.

"Shouldn't you be on the other side of the grounds with the rest of the girls?"

I never liked bullies, especially this kid.

"Shouldn't you be back in the zoo with the rest of your family?" I yelled back.

He came at me, and I tackled him. We wrestled to the ground. Fists flew. I got the best of him just before a priest jumped in to break us up. We were both sent to the principal's office, but nobody teased me from that day forward. I had established a reputation as someone you didn't mess with, someone who had a quick temper and was kind of crazy. You never knew what I might do.

The bullying and teasing reminded me of the same reaction after my first Halloween. This accelerated the denial of my true self. An endless cycle of denial, followed by lukewarm acceptance, then back to denial, would be my pattern for many years to come.

You can run from something for much of your life, but not all of it. Eventually, truth overcomes false appearances, and the pretender within you dies. I desperately wanted to be myself, but remained conflicted about allowing that to happen. My only hope for finding reconciliation was from within, but many things in the world around me would have to change first.

Chapter Two:
Good Catholic Boy

I was late for school again. Last year, my tardiness had more than once resulted in Saturday detention. This year was no different — in fact, my interest in school had declined even further.

I shook the sleepiness from my head and grabbed a clean uniform. Considering how I felt about boys' clothes in general, my school uniform might as well have had a prisoner's name tag and number. I pulled on the stiff corduroy pants that never fit well and did not allow air flow to critical areas. I often joked with classmates that severe chafing was their intended purpose, by order of the Archbishop of Extreme Discomfort.

I buttoned up the white Oxford shirt with long sleeves and button-down collar that had to be starched to the point that it could stand in a corner by itself if so ordered. The ensemble was completed with a dark green tie that choked you when pulled to its required tightness. All in all, the uniform represented the conformist, disciplined constraints of the Catholic grade school that constantly imposed a definition of who I should and should not be.

Today felt particularly torturous. Late September in Minneapolis could go either way: there might be frost on the ground and fall's chill in the air, or summer could linger into October with uncomfortable heat and heavy, wet air. This day was the latter, hot and humid.

As I closed the front door and descended the front steps, I fell into a familiar fantasy. What if a swarm of corduroy-eating giant moths with an appetite for poorly designed, ill-fitting clothing attacked and consumed my uniform? I would be given a girl's uniform in its place, since there was nothing else available. No one could fault me. I was doing what I was told, right? At twelve years of age, I hung onto whatever I could for relief.

Summer was on life support, its final breaths labored. The half-green leaves resisted their inevitable transformation, slowly turning shades of orange, red, and yellow. In our predominantly Catholic neighborhood, families were large. Some had as many as twelve children. I was the youngest of eight. Everyone went to the same grade school, and most lived within walking distance. The sidewalks were normally crowded with uniformed parochial kids, making room for more who ran down the front steps to join them for the short walk. The usual chasing, teasing, and calling out to friends went on all the way to school, then the noise ceased as everyone became serious and quiet upon arrival.

But today I was so late that the sidewalks were empty and the houses quiet. It was strange to be alone on the way to school without a kid to be seen anywhere. You would have thought a tornado warning had gone off and everyone had evacuated.

Arriving at school, I was sweating bullets. The second I was inside, I yanked at my shirt, untucking it for a bit of relief. I didn't care about the dress code at that point and headed up the staircase towards my second-floor homeroom. Reaching the top, I paused to catch my breath. Bent over with my hands on my thighs, I gasped for air. As I stood upright, I could see a figure at the opposite end of the long, silent hallway.

As she approached, I heard the familiar clicking of beads colliding with metal crosses and the rustling layers of a floor-length tunic in harmonic symphony. I always made fun of the nuns who were fully decked out in extra battle gear. I told my pals that the longer beaded rosaries and heavy crucifixes draped from their multiple layers of habit were indications of greater authority. They were the four-star nuns — generals, battle-tested by years of survival within the Catholic hierarchy. They were the enforcers, best suited to be the school's disciplinarians.

As she closed the distance between us, I could finally make out the nun's features, and my fears were confirmed. I turned to walk in the opposite direction.

"Stop right there, Michael."

The hair on my neck stood up as her voice echoed through the empty hallway: Sister Mary Bartholomew — or, as I called her, Sister Mary Discipline.

"To my office now, Michael."

Bridging the distance between us, she placed her hand on my upper back and prodded me back down the hall. Inside her office, she sat behind her desk and pointed to the chair opposite hers.

"Sit."

Complying, I sat and watched her stern face carefully for signs of life. No eye movement or expressions, just stone cold, but that was purposeful. She lived to strike fear into the hearts of unruly grade-schoolers. She placed her reading glasses on the bridge of her nose and looked at me through them. Turning in her chair, she reached into a file cabinet and retrieved a folder with my name on the index tab. You knew you'd been in trouble too many times when they had a folder just for you. She looked up at me over her glasses, then back down again at the file.

"You are off to an early start down the wrong path this year, Michael."

I remained silent and expressionless, giving no indication of fear or concern.

"You have a history of tardiness and many violations of the dress code. How many times must you be reminded that shirttails are to remain tucked into your pants?"

Not thinking my reply would upset her, I said, "This is my first late this year."

She threw her hands up in the air as if I'd scored a touchdown.

"Congratulations, your first! Does that mean there will be more to follow?"

"No, I will be on time from now on, really I will."

She bent over the file to analyze further.

"Your behavior over the last two years has given me no reason to believe you have or will make any attempt at repentance. I have called your mother more than once to discuss the changes in your attitude. Neither one of us can figure out why you are acting out and not completing your schoolwork."

She looked up at me and sighed as though all hope was lost.

"I have seen a young boy who was a straight 'A' student turn into an unruly, distracted one whose grades are going down. A boy who only seems interested in sports, fighting, and being the class clown. Why do you take it upon yourself to entertain your classmates and distract them from their work? A good Catholic boy does not behave in this manner."

I sat silently for a minute, absorbing all of that. She had no way of knowing what I was going through. She couldn't possibly know that my clown suit was my armor. It shielded me against being seen for who I was on the inside, the real me that I could never reveal. I had learned early in life that if I was funny, I would be liked. If I were tough, I'd be feared; if I excelled in sports, I'd be respected.

The truthful answer to her question was that I worked harder on my reputation and hiding who I was than I did on my schoolwork; something I have since regretted for my entire life.

"I don't know, Sister. I just do these things."

"Yes, you do, and let's talk about some of those things."

Elbows on her desk, hands folded, she gazed at the file again. What else could be in there? Was I really that awful?

"Let's begin with the comic strips you somehow found time to draw in class and pass around. Your classmates were amused by the unflattering satire of priests, nuns, and other authorities, but your teachers found them offensive and sacrilegious."

"Yes, I remember serving detention and paying penance for that."

"To my point. You do remember, but you are not learning from your bad acts, because here we are once again in my office."

Looking up, she grumbled, "Orange hair, really? What was that about?"

"That was a big mistake, Sister."

"I'll say, and what was the mistake?"

"It was supposed to be blonde."

"I see. So, it was only a poor color choice?"

"No, it was foolish. I heard that if you put peroxide in your hair, it would turn blonde, and I thought that would be cool. I put it on before bed. When I woke up, I had orange hair! My Mom told me I had to live with the consequences, and I would have to go to school that way. I did, and took all the teasing. My Dad shaved my head after that, and I had a whole new look."

"We know that. It was all one big distraction to everyone."

Rising from her chair, she opened a cabinet behind her and retrieved something I couldn't see.

"Perhaps what you need is a more memorable lesson this time. I cannot have you walking around these halls with your shirt tails hanging out like you own the place."

I didn't know what to expect next, but it didn't sound good.

"Come over here and stand next to me, Michael, and turn around."

I could now see that in her hand was an extra-wide roll of pink lace.

"Now hold still and you won't get stuck."

Unravelling the roll, she pinned the lace to the bottom of my untucked shirt.

Turning me slowly, she created a multi-tiered pink lace hem, making the shirt appear like a lace-trimmed dress.

"Perfect."

She was smiling, sure that I would be ashamed.

"If you are going to wear your shirt out and look girlish, it might as well be a dress."

She was determined to humiliate me, but had no way of knowing that I loved pink lace and dresses. How appropriate that she converted my drab, starched shirt into a cute pink dress!

My face turned red, but not from embarrassment. It was pure joy, and an attempt to contain my laughter. This wasn't punishment, it was fun. The joke was on her.

"You are not to remove this lace for the remainder of the day. You will bring it back to me, still on, at day's end. There is a general assembly in the auditorium in five minutes. You will go directly there and take your assigned seat with the rest of your class. You won't seem so clever to your little followers now. They'll be laughing *at* you, not *with* you."

What a cruel expectation. I wasn't about to let her get the satisfaction of making me ashamed of myself in front of everyone. I was determined to turn this around on her.

"Next time you will remember, yes?"

"Yes, Sister."

"Now go, or you'll be late again today."

I headed toward the auditorium, which was not far from her lair.

Kids poured out of their classrooms and down the hall in tight single-file ranks as instructed. I tried to find a place in line but was kept out by the kids' pace and tight formation. I was more noticeable to everyone as we approached the room. Soon, kids were laughing at me and jeering.

Almost everyone was already seated by the time I reached the auditorium. It was time for me to take control. I strutted into the room confidently, taking long, exaggerated strides like a runway model. My movements were self-mocking as I blew kisses to my audience and did 'parade queen' hand waves.

I won them over. The jeers became cheers, whistles of encouragement, and applause. Reaching the aisle of my seat, I did a 360 spin, curtsied in each direction, and took my seat. Now they're laughing *with* me, not *at* me, Sister. I thought I had won the day, until I looked across the room. Leaning against the far wall, glaring at me with her arms folded tightly, was Sister Mary Discipline. When she caught my gaze, she pointed directly at me and motioned for me to come her way.

The following Saturday, I was the only student serving detention. The solitude was supposed to give you time to reflect on your transgressions while clearing blackboards of chalk and pounding erasers. It worked as intended. Thinking about how I ended up in school on a Saturday while my friends enjoyed their freedom had me considering my actions. I knew I'd been wrong to make a mockery of my punishment while in assembly, but I also knew the Sister was wrong to teach me a lesson through humiliation.

The thing that troubled me, however, was what she had been right about. She struck a deep nerve when she mentioned how I had changed and that she couldn't figure out why I'd become disconnected from my studies and responsibilities.

I had changed. I was heading into puberty and didn't understand my thoughts and feelings towards my own gender. I was confused and acted out with irreverence and disrespect. Inside, I was frightened. What kind of life would be ahead of me if I had to hide who I was and how I felt?

My body was beginning to change. I had seen my older brothers grow mustaches, become taller, and more muscular. I didn't want that for myself. I knew I would become more and more male as time passed. There was no stopping or changing what was coming. I was dreading the very thing all boys my age couldn't wait for: becoming a young man. Sister Bartholomew was trying to save me from myself, but there wasn't enough pink lace in the world to alter the path I was on.

Chapter Three: One of the Boys

I've never figured out how my Mom and Dad survived raising eight children while operating a small restaurant that required a minimum twelve-hour workday.

By the time my oldest brother and three sisters were out of the house, my parents were still left with me and three older brothers at home. The four of us were separated by a total of only seven years. We were very close-knit.

My Mom must have dreaded when our home phone rang. It was often a teacher from one of our schools or a neighbor complaining about something one of us had done. If it was something worth telling my Dad about, she would call him at the restaurant. You were in real trouble when that occurred, and you usually heard, "Wait until your father gets home."

If you happened to be working at the restaurant (which we all were) at the time, and you knew it was Mom calling, it was not going to be good. Dad always answered the phone the same way: "Louie's Kitchen." If he remained silent, there was trouble ahead.

The long pause was a dead giveaway: "Uh-huh, yeah, he did what?" The next thing out of his mouth was usually a loud, drawn-out "JEEEEZUS H. CHRIST!" I never knew why he added the H or what it meant, but I was smart enough not to ask. Once in a while, he'd yell, "JEEEEZUS BALLS," and I'd stifle my laughter and leave the room.

What kept us out of trouble most of the time, though, was our love of sports. We loved competition and played any sport any time we had a chance. Often, we'd split up and play against each other in two-on-two games. We were in our glory when we were able to play on the same team.

Our level of competition would be highest when we played another competitive family or group of friends, and I always found it necessary to go all-out in order to prove myself to my brothers.

My over-compensation usually meant I was throwing my body around with reckless abandon, resulting in cuts and bruises. I didn't care why I did this at the time, but I now realize I was covering up my deeper issues.

When there wasn't a ballfield available at the park, we would go to a local schoolyard that was paved over and fenced in. It made a perfect baseball field... except for its hard surface.

One day, we were challenged by a group of kids we didn't know very well, but they knew us by our reputation.

We played a hard-fought game that came down to the last out. Their guy hit a ball my way in left field that appeared out of reach and would drop in for a hit. I left my feet, extended my body out, sliding on the asphalt, and I caught the ball to end the game.

As I got up and shoved my glove into the air to show I caught it, I could see blood dripping down from my elbows, and my pants were ripped at the knees. I was smiling from ear to ear.

"Game over!" I shouted.

One of the kids walked up to my brother as we shook hands and said, "Good game, but your fucking brother is crazy!"

"Maybe, but did you see that catch?"

I was pleased when I heard that. The competitor in me loved winning, but if I made my brothers proud, it was that much sweeter.

We all had our own friends our age, but the times we spent together were special. I was able to distract myself from my personal problems as long as I had my family, at an age when I was young enough not to let anything bother me too much, and we were all still living at home.

When I was busy with family, the voice in my head was muted. I would forget myself and just enjoy our time together. Alone, however, my thoughts were loud and clear. I was confused and puzzled by what my inner self desired.

Chapter Four: Growing Pained

My heart raced as I ran to the upstairs bathroom and locked the door behind me. Our large Minneapolis house was eerily quiet when no one else was home. Every sound was conspicuous. I'd heard a door slam and wasn't sure if it came from inside or outside. I wasn't taking any chances.

I kept quiet, listening for footsteps, any sound, for what seemed like hours before I slowly opened the bathroom door and stepped lightly across the hardwood floor to minimize squeaking.

The skirt I had struggled to get into was too tight. It hobbled me as I clumsily made my way to the front bedroom. I side-stepped along the walls to avoid being seen from the front windows. I leaned in slightly, scanning up and down the street. There were no cars in front of our house, but I noticed the neighbor across the street unloading groceries from her car. She slammed her trunk, making the same noise I'd heard a few minutes earlier.

I felt the tension in my shoulders ease, and made my way back to the bathroom. I was short of breath from excitement. Looking into the mirror above the vanity, I noticed my flushed-red face.

It was humiliating to find myself in this position once again. Though I was rarely home alone, whenever I was, I took advantage of it by finding ways to feed my need to be a girl. I'd pull on my sisters' discarded sweaters or skirts they'd put away in drawers. Sometimes I'd rummage in the attic for Mom's old dresses. These brief sessions always ended the same way: I would hear noises, scurry to take things off, put them away, and hope I didn't get caught.

Once, not long before this episode, one of my brothers came home from school early, and I was caught off guard. I ran up the steps to the attic, tripping on my skirt as I tried to remove it.

He heard the noise from downstairs and yelled, "Who's upstairs? Is that you, Mike?"

I ran back down into the bathroom, putting my clothes on. I flushed the toilet a few times and sprayed air freshener, pretending to mask a foul odor that didn't exist.

"Yeah, I'm in the bathroom. I'd stay out of here if I were you. I've got really bad diarrhea."

He came halfway up the stairs and stared at me as I came out into the hallway.

"Why is your face so red?"

"I'm not sure. I think I might have a fever. I'm going to lie down for a while."

"Damn, you make a lot of noise when you're sick."

"Why do you think they call it the runs?" I said, trying to lighten the moment.

"Right, funny," he said, turning to head back downstairs.

Now, I examined my red face in the mirror. I poked a finger into the flesh of my cheek. When I hit puberty, I'd gained 25 pounds. It was getting harder to find any clothing to wear. Just half an hour ago, I'd struggled getting into my favorite blue skirt. Now, it was difficult to pull down over my enlarged waist. When it finally fell to my ankles, I noticed the zipper had torn away from its seam.

Remembering a time when it fit, I was filled with disgust. I was so much taller and heavier. My facial hair was coming in, male equipment was developing, and my voice had gotten deeper. Still gazing into the mirror, I could only see a fat fourteen-year-old boy pathetically attempting to be something that was now far beyond reach.

I folded the skirt neatly, hiding the torn zipper, and put it back in my sister's old room. What was I going to do? There would be no relief without this outlet. I had no space to be myself. But who was I?

The Uninvited Passenger

I stared into the bathroom mirror again. My mind flooded with bleak visions of the future. Was this what the rest of my life was? Would all my days ahead be filled with frustration, unfulfilled hope, and self-hatred? I was sick of holding back who I was, but the truth was evident. Every effort I made to be a girl now would end in futility. As a child, I had always been able to imagine worlds where I could express myself openly. Now I'd lost all hope.

As if in a dream, I opened the medicine cabinet next to the vanity. A prescription medicine bottle with a toxic warning label on the side facing me stood out as a personal invitation. Mom's name was printed on the label, along with the instructions: TAKE ONLY AS PRESCRIBED BY YOUR DOCTOR. TAKING MORE THAN THE PRESCRIBED DOSAGE COULD BE FATAL. I held the bottle for a moment, then threw back several into my mouth. I cupped my hands under the cold-water faucet and sipped enough to chase them down. I walked over to the toilet, sat down, and put my head in my hands. I had no idea what was coming next, or how quickly it would happen.

Suddenly, I was scared. What had I just done? I love my family, I thought. I can't do this to them. I love my God, and this goes against everything I believe in. I love my friends, music, and sports. There are things in my life more important than my feelings! I can't let this happen. I got up from the toilet and paced around the hallway. What was I going to do? Did I need to call someone for help?

Just then, I heard the front door open. Mom was home from her day's work at our family restaurant. My stomach felt queasy as I rushed down the stairs. Mom laid her coat over the back of the sofa.

"You look pale. Are you okay?" she asked.

"I'm not sure, Mom. I took some pills that weren't what I thought, and now my stomach hurts," I said sheepishly.

She reached over, placing both hands on my shoulders and pulling me towards her.

"What? How long ago and what did you take?"

"Just a few minutes ago. The bottle is upstairs by the medicine cabinet. I thought they were vitamins, but now I'm not sure."

She ran up the stairs, pulling me behind.

"Get up here right now and show me exactly what you took."

I followed her upstairs. The pill bottle was sitting on the sink.

"Is this what you took?"

"Yes."

"This is my medication. Don't you know well enough to read the label before taking something, especially a prescription that is clearly marked?"

I stood silent. I knew that question didn't require an answer.

"Let's get you down to the kitchen and take care of this," she said.

She prodded me to the stairs and we hurried to the kitchen.

"You're not going to like this, but you need to hold your head over the sink and do as I tell you."

"Okay, Mom," I said, not knowing what I was in for.

She reached under the sink and grabbed a bottle of liquid dish soap, squirted it into a glass, then added water from the spout.

"Put your head back and open your mouth as wide as you can. Drink this until you start throwing up."

I opened it wide. She poured the warm, soapy water down my throat. My gag reflex went into action immediately, and I dry-heaved several times before finally hitting the gusher. The contents of my stomach were now in the sink. The pills were whole and undigested.

"Good! Now let's make sure we got all of them out."

Gasping for air, barely able to speak, I said, "No, no, Mom. I'm sure we got them all."

"You can't be sure. You told me you weren't sure how many you took."

Quickly, I counted the pills in the sink.

"Seven, I took seven!"

She pulled my head back and poured the next batch down my throat while I squirmed in her grasp.

"Let's just be sure we have them all out. You put yourself in this mess, now you have to pay the consequences."

Consequences, always those damned consequences! It seemed like lately, I was always getting in trouble for things outside of my control. That batch made me gag several more times without producing anything from my stomach. All it did was make my throat burn more. I was relieved, though. There couldn't possibly be a pill left in me.

She pulled a chair out from under the kitchen table. "Sit down for a minute," she said.

Weak in the knees, I made it to the table.

"Do you feel better now?"

"I'm glad that's over, but no, I'm not really feeling very well right now."

"Well, that's good. You need to remember how this feels and how sick you could get from taking pills that belong to someone else. You are old enough to know better. If you want vitamins, you need to read those labels! The ones we have are ONE-A-DAY brand. That's all you need to take, not a handful."

"I get it, Mom. I'm sorry. I'll be more careful."

"God, I hope so. You scared the holy hell out of me."

Lying down in my room after that long afternoon, I was astounded that I'd gone so far as to try to kill myself. I had let my feelings override my common sense. There had to be a better way to deal with the festering sore in my conscious being.

Dad always said, "Keep your hands on the wheel and eyes on the road. You need to concentrate on what's important."

I had to focus on the positive. I would do better, for the time being.

The next year was my freshman year of high school. Like all of my brothers before me, I enrolled in the same Catholic school. It was an all-boys school run by an all-male faculty and administration. The teachers were Christian Brothers who were devoted to their faith and to educating their students. They were also strict disciplinarians who molded young boys into young men. This shone a bright light on my fraudulent maleness. Classrooms, hallways, assembly rooms, gymnasiums, all with nothing but boys and men. Being without the presence of girls or women did not appeal to me. I was a fish out of water. I hated every minute of every day. I was at odds with everyone around me from the start.

Only a few weeks in, I couldn't take any more. I showed up for homeroom attendance, then cut class. Soon after, I was called to the disciplinary brother's office. His solution to my problem was to have me sit in his waiting room and copy the entire Bible in my handwriting. This punishment lasted all of two hours before I got up and walked out. I knew how to take a hint.

For the first time in my life, I was relegated to public schools. The one I could get into in our district on short notice was the toughest in the city. The students seemed to be running the show, but I was able to make it through the year without getting into trouble.

The following year, I was allowed to transfer to a better school closer to our family restaurant, since I worked there. At my new school, I did my best to fit in at first. I was sixteen. My dysphoria intensified, along with more physical changes. My emotional and mental state now conflicted entirely with my body. The fact that I still thought of myself as a girl, but was attracted to them, compounded my confusion. I recall my embarrassment in a Q&A discussion held in the auditorium. I was seated next to a very attractive girl, and she accidentally rubbed against me. I was immediately aroused and prayed that I wasn't called upon to stand up and give my opinion. I was ashamed of myself. What was this body doing?

Those inner contradictions made it difficult to approach girls or ask them out for a date. I became shy around them, fearing they sensed my femininity. I didn't go on my first date until I was nineteen.

I kept myself busy. I had a job after school and worked at the family restaurant as well. I was able to afford my first car at sixteen. That made me popular, but not with the 'popular' kids. I suspected some had similar troubles, but were afraid to tell anyone, just as I was. Life is hard enough as a teenager; no one wants to add to that mess!

There was an unspoken understanding among my friends that we were all out of the mainstream, which is why we hung out together. We felt safe and comfortable with each other, but never to the point of disclosing our difficulties. I could never reveal my gender identity, even to my best friends, for fear that I would have no friends at all. My friends were not the 'A' students or student body leaders. Nope — we were proud to see ourselves as outcasts and rebels, always finding some kind of trouble.

I fooled myself into believing that my gender problems would disappear with time, or that I would simply 'grow out of them.' But nothing would be that simple in my life.

I could only grip the wheel tighter and focus my eyes on the road ahead.

Chapter Five:
Arrested Development

In my late teenage years, I reached the peak of my dysphoria. My physical changes weighed heavily on me. I saw the finality of never being able to do anything about this. I was desperate to make changes that did not exist for me. I needed help, but I didn't know where to find it. The truth was too raw and painful. I was on a downward spiral.

It is amazing to me how people of like minds find each other: positives attract while negatives collide. I was still making friends, but now they were increasingly the kids that my parents had so wisely suggested I avoid. The crowd I ran with included Jeff, a friend from grade school whom I had reconnected with recently. Jeff had been in and out of trouble since high school. He was a small-time marijuana dealer who had done time in juvenile detention. He was always willing to share with us. Jeff's older brother John had just returned from a stint in a state prison, and Jeff followed his brother's lead much of the time.

The Uninvited Passenger

Then there was my friend Pat's older brother. He had just returned from a tour of duty in Vietnam, where he had become addicted to amphetamines. He shared the blue pills from his stash with us a few times, but I hated the way I felt when I came crashing down from the high. Still, I couldn't escape the constant flow of weed, speed, and alcohol that was available wherever I went. I knew I had lost control of myself, but could not put the brakes on. Previously, my better judgment had warned me when to stop, but now the green light was on, and I was agreeing to things I would not have in the past.

On a grim, dark November day, it was colder than usual, with the bitterness of winter in the air. We were in Pat's basement smoking a joint. My mood was as dark as the weather.

"Hey, come on, man, cheer up," Pat said, "Jeff is on his way over and he wants us to come with him. He said we could score some easy money."

"Score some money, how?" I asked.

Pat took another hit off the joint. "Not sure, but it's a piece of cake."

"No such thing," I replied.

"Well, this one is," Pat said with certainty, "This dude owes Jeff's brother money, and we're going to his house to pick it up. Jeff just needs us for backup."

"Jeff's brother John," I accepted the joint and inhaled, "if he's coming, I'm not."

Pat was sure it was a safe play. "John's not coming. He can't be taking chances on parole, so Jeff's handling this."

I should have cared enough to ask more questions, but I was high and it seemed like easy money.

"All right. I'm in."

Jeff popped his head through Pat's basement window about a half-hour later.

"You guys ready to do this?"

In the car, Jeff was silent and dead serious. We'd only gone a few blocks from Pat's and were close to where I lived.

"Whose house is this?" I asked as we pulled up.

"A guy my brother knows. Don't worry about it," Jeff said quietly.

"What am I supposed to do here?" I asked.

"You guys wait here while I see what's going on inside. Keep the car ready to go, and watch for anyone."

I was sobering up now, and my natural suspicion returned. My house was a few blocks from here, I thought; maybe I should just walk home. Instead, I watched Jeff climb the stairs to the house, which was hidden from the street by trees and hedges. After a few minutes, Jeff finally appeared at the top of the hill, waving his arms and signaling me up to the house.

As I stepped through the side door, Jeff frantically handed me wads of cash and jewelry he had taken from inside somewhere. Without thinking, I stuffed them into a bag that was on the landing.

"Take this. There's more upstairs, and they're worth cash," he said as he shoved the butt end of a handgun towards me. I'd never had a gun in my hands in my life, and now I was stealing one? The whole thing felt like a movie I was watching. What was I doing?

"Where the fuck is Pat going?"

Jeff's voice startled me. He had seen Pat's car speed away from the front window.

"Let's get the hell out of here, Jeff. Pat bolted. He must've seen someone coming," I shouted back in a panic.

Jeff hurried down the stairs as I ran out the side door to head through the backyard. I realized I had a gun on me and would be considered armed, whether it was mine or not. I heaved the weapon as far as I could into the hedges.

A police officer came at me from the front yard, and another from the alley I had hoped to use as an escape route. I was trapped. With my hands high in the air, I turned towards the police officer coming at me from the backyard.

"Hands on top of your head, get down on your knees, don't move!"

As I complied, he got behind me, pulled my hands down behind my back, and cuffed me all in one motion, with such force that I thought he had broken my arm.

"Hey man, take it easy! I'm not armed. That gun came from inside the house."

I turned my head slightly, trying to look at him, but he pushed my head away. I could feel the barrel of his gun against my neck.

"I told you not to move."

He pressed his gun harder against my skin.

"Okay, okay," I replied, my voice shaking. I was frightened enough that he had his gun pointed at me. Now I felt the cold barrel, and the fear traveled up my spine. Another police officer had retrieved the gun I'd tossed aside and held it out where I could see it.

"This your gun, tough guy?"

"No, it came from the house."

"Shut the fuck up, I didn't want an answer," he snapped back. He pulled me off my knees and frisked me.

"Any more weapons on you, badass?"

I kept my mouth shut, thinking that anything I said would cause more problems.

"He's clean, let's go."

They both grabbed me and led me to the squad car, shoving me down by the top of my head into the back seat.

I could see Jeff already subdued in the back of another squad as I was being read my rights.

Being handcuffed in the back of a police car on my way to the downtown Minneapolis precinct was beyond anything I could have imagined in my worst nightmare. The events of the day had unfolded so quickly. Why did I listen to Pat and get in his car? How come he got away when he'd been the one who talked me into this? Where were my better instincts, the ones that had always led me away from this kind of trouble? This was not like getting suspended from school. This was very real and deeply serious.

A million things were going through my head at once. More than anything else, I could not stop thinking about what this would do to my parents. My dad would be heartbroken that I had become a criminal. Mom would be devastated and ashamed. I could bear the thought of jail time, but not what I had just done to Mom and Dad. How could I ever face them?

It got dark early this time of year, and the streetlights had just come on. The Minneapolis Police headquarters was located within a multi-purpose municipal building, which was home to all City and County government offices, including the courts and jails. It was a mammoth Romanesque fortress: a striking, seven-story structure taking up four square city blocks and constructed of dark rose granite. The steep, green copper roofs and spires were accentuated by a high clock tower featuring a four-sided clock 25 feet across. At night, it appeared medieval. On this particular evening, it was suitably haunting.

We drove into the belly of the beast, down an entrance ramp that took us below street level into a secure area. I was transported to central booking, where I was officially charged with a crime, photographed, and fingerprinted. There were others waiting to be booked. I couldn't believe I was in their company. How had I suddenly become a criminal? I'd never been in serious trouble before. This was going to be a long night with many long days to follow. I had to reach inside myself to find stamina. I had never felt this alone.

I was taken to the detective unit and made to wait for what seemed like hours. Finally, a robbery and burglary detective arrived and sat across from me. He reviewed some paperwork, then looked at me directly and said, "I'm the detective assigned to your case. I've already interviewed your pal, and I have to say, we can connect you to more than what you were arrested for today — and send you up to the Cloud for an exceptionally long time."

The Cloud was Saint Cloud State Prison. I knew of it from all the older guys in our neighborhood who had disappeared into the Cloud. I kept my mouth shut as he paused, waiting for a reaction.

"I see this is your first offense, but I think it's just the first time you've been caught."

I had to respond to that absurdity: "It is the first time I have been caught and the only time I have done anything like this."

"I'm not believing you because your partner has a brother who's been in the Cloud, and his known associates have as well."

"What's that have to do with me or this?" I fired back.

"What does that have to do with you? This looks like an organized crime ring to me. A bunch of street-smart adults running a group of younger punks to steal for them while they accept the stolen property and sell it off."

"No, that's not what happened here, or any other time I know about."

"So you say, but that's not what we believe — and will prove," he said confidently. "Unless you identify the driver of the getaway car."

Now I saw what he was after. I was in this fix because of my bad choices, but I saw no reason to ruin Pat's life as well. I was not going to rat him out.

"There was no driver. No car, just us on foot all the way."

"Bullshit," he shot back, "That's what your partner in crime said too."

"So our stories are the same. We didn't have time to rehearse. It must be true."

He moved his chair closer to stare me down.

"So, you guys are protecting the same asshole that was supposed to be the lookout but fled the scene like a coward, leaving you hanging? What a couple of idiots. You know the reason you're sitting here," he said, sounding incredulous, "Because a watchful neighbor saw the car running out front with a guy sitting in it and called us. Your pal decided to save his own ass and got you arrested!"

"I don't know who you're referring to," I replied.

"Man! You guys watch too much television. This is real shit you're in, and you better knock off the bravado or you are going to do serious time!"

Sounded to me like he was the one who watched too much television. I was waiting for his partner to come in and do the good cop/bad cop routine. He got up from his chair and slammed it back under the table.

"Okay, you made another bad choice today. If this is the story you're staying with, then my report will include every asshole thief in South Minneapolis and connect you with them, whether you know them or not. If you're banking on a light sentence because you just turned eighteen and this is your first arrest, forget about that. I will make sure the Minneapolis prosecutor's office is aware that you are a part of this syndicate."

Syndicate? No way he could link me with people I had no connection to. He was angry because I wouldn't tell him what he wanted to hear, so he was going to destroy me. I knew I'd messed up big time, but I also knew I hadn't been involved in any other crime, ever. I was getting pissed off, which strengthened my resolve.

"It's the way it happened," I said firmly.

"Okay. I will make my recommendation to the prosecutor's office." He turned, shuffled his papers, and flung the door open. "Enjoy your weekend, because you're going to be here until Monday at least. Bail hearings are done for the day, and bail bonds people are gone for the weekend, too."

A guard entered the room and took me to an area where I was further searched, stripped, and given my jailhouse attire: an ill-fitting jumpsuit, just what I needed to make me look the part of the fool I had become. As he escorted me to the jail, my fear resurfaced. The general lockup area was vast and painted in bleak battleship grey. I was just old enough to be tossed in with the adults. I wanted to get to my cell and be locked in.

Buzzed in beyond the large steel barricade door, we entered a long corridor lined on either side with cells. As I was escorted towards my cell, I could see Jeff across the hall in the other block. He was within earshot, but even if I'd been able to call out to him, what would I have said?

My own cell was a relief until I tried getting comfortable. I had only a small cot consisting of a thin mat on top of a web of metal springs, a low-rider toilet, and a small sink. I realized I hadn't eaten since early that morning. Dinner time had come and gone in the cell block, and no one was offering anything.

This was jail, not a hotel. The guy who showed me to my room was not my bellman, nor was the guard up front the concierge service. I was here of my own doing, and I *should* go without dinner, I thought to myself.

Gazing at the faces of those around me, I realized I was fortunate to be locked in my own cell. I was conspicuously the youngest here and incredibly vulnerable. I would not be seeing anyone from my family that night. It was late, and there would be no visitors.

"Lights out in ten minutes, followed by complete silence," the guard said.

The lights did go out, but the silence did not occur. Obscenities were shouted back and forth by inmates who had issues. I just wanted them to shut up so I could rest my brain. My head was throbbing as I lay on the scratchy wool blanket. I had finally fallen asleep when I heard clanging above my head and was startled to see a guard standing on top of the cage, beating on the bars with his club.

"What's wrong, Princess? Can't sleep? You need your teddy bear?"

God damn it! Was everybody in this building a complete asshole? Why was the guy taunting me? What a sick son of a bitch! He moved down the line, selectively harassing other inmates until he tired of it.

Finally, I fell asleep for a few hours. I awakened before dawn, thinking I was in a bad dream, but soon realized this was for real. I could not fall asleep again. I worried about my family and if they knew where I was. I was told they would be called, but I didn't trust anyone here after what I'd experienced since my arrest.

Chapter Six:
Saturday Morning in Jail

My first night in jail was not a restful one. I awakened to shouts from several inmates that echoed through the cellblock and bounced around in my head. Soon after, the sound level died down as the guards approached the cells with carts carrying the morning meal. Nothing like feeding time at the zoo to calm the inhabitants.

I hadn't eaten for a day and wasn't concerned about what was being served. I would eat what they put in front of me. A guard rolled a cart into the common area, handing out trays to each prisoner as he worked his way past each cell. Taking mine, I removed the plastic cover and ate what appeared to be powdered eggs, a meat-like substance, and very dry toast. If being incarcerated for a crime was not enough of a deterrent, the food certainly drove home the "crime doesn't pay" theme.

As the morning went on, visitors were brought in and allowed to see the prisoners through the bars. Speaking from the corridor, most kept their voices lowered for privacy, while others were unconcerned. When your visitor arrived, a guard announced your name and said, "Visitor coming!"

There were few arrivals until early afternoon, when I heard Jeff's name called, followed by "visitor coming."

Jeff's dad appeared in the corridor. He swayed in front of Jeff's cell, then grabbed the bars before unloading on Jeff. He was staggering drunk.

"Jeffrey, I told you that I would see you in jail one day, and here you are!"

He didn't bother to keep his voice down. I was certain everyone in the cellblock heard him.

"You're as worthless as your god damned brother and twice as stupid!"

Jeff hung his head. His body slumped against the bars of his cell as his dad continued to humiliate him publicly.

"If it weren't for your mother, I would let your ass rot down here as long as they want to keep you, but I guess I'll have to make your god damned bail and drag your sorry ass back home."

I knew Jeff's dad was a drunk, angry man, but I thought he would show a little compassion at a time when his son was most vulnerable.

After Jeff's dad left, I had a few hours to think about my own fate. I imagined how I would react to seeing my own dad from behind bars. I felt guilty about his having to make the trip downtown from his restaurant. Dad would have to close early to make it during visiting hours. I wasn't worried about him yelling at me; that's not how he dealt with things. I was more concerned about looking him in the eyes, facing up to what I had done. I knew he would be deeply disappointed in me, and that was enough to make me feel like a complete asshole.

I tried not to think about it. The afternoon was dragging on when I heard my name called out and "visitor coming." My heart now in my throat, I stepped into the common area and over to the bars where I could see my dad getting closer. I could see the weariness in his face and sadness in his eyes.

"Listen," he said when he stood facing me. "I don't know what brought you to this point. This is not you. You're better than the guy I am looking at behind these bars."

I felt the weight lift off my shoulders and drew a deep breath.

"I'm sorry, Dad. I don't know how things got so far away from me, but I put myself in this mess and–"

He stopped me mid-sentence and moved in closer. Eyes fixed on mine, he spoke with resolve and compassion.

"What matters right here and now is that you understand: I am behind you 100 percent and we will get through this together."

I teared up thinking about Jeff's dad a few hours before, and how lucky I was to have a dad like mine. He had every reason to be just as upset, but chose to love and support me in a time of my greatest despair.

"Look," he said, squeezing my hand firmly through the bars, "You had to be out of your senses to do this, out on a lark with your buddies. Regardless, this is serious trouble, and you're going to have to face the consequences for your actions, but you won't be doing it alone."

I pulled myself together enough to ask a question I knew the answer to.

"How's Mom doing?"

He looked down at the floor. "She's upset, angry, disappointed, but she's also worried about you."

"Tell her I'm sorry."

"You can tell her yourself when we get you bailed out on Monday. But in the meantime, just know both of us are with you and will be all the way."

"Thanks, Dad."

"I have to get home and let her know you're okay. Keep your head up."

Things could have gone another way, but my Dad's reassurance gave me the fortitude to get through the weekend and go from there.

The rest of the weekend, I had a lot of time to think about the last couple of years of my life: where I had abandoned myself and lost interest in my own well-being. If my Dad could handle all the problems in his life and remain focused, reasonable, and caring, couldn't I put more effort into getting my own shit together? No more weed or drinking. I needed to straighten out everything in my life that I had control over, and a few things that I did not. I vowed to focus only on bettering myself as a human being.

Chapter Seven: Storms of Change

---•---

A long, stubborn winter finally gave way to the anticipated change of season. With the promise of renewal, springtime brought relief from the dreariness. Along with the seasonal change came my court disposition. Fortunately, I was placed on probation and avoided prison time.

Following the rules of probation, I had a full-time job with help from the probation officer's job placement program. I was following the rules to the letter, but I hated the work. I was placed in a screw machine shop, operating a semi-automated machine that required hands-on contact all day, loading and unloading parts as they were machined in a constant bath of oil as the equipment droned on. There was an oil guard on the machine, but it was useless. By the day's end, I was soaked in machine oil, and my clothes stuck to my skin. The smell and taste of it never left my nostrils or mouth. It paid well and kept me out of trouble, but it was monotonous and filthy. It seemed a gloomy dead-end.

Our home life had changed over the last couple of years, changed so much. All my siblings were married and living elsewhere. The house was now occupied by Mom, Dad, and me. It was so quiet and different from how I grew up. Dad had gotten out of the restaurant business and was working for someone else for less income. The time had come to sell the big family house in the city. Mom hated the idea of leaving her beautiful old home with all its charming woodwork and custom finishings. She would miss her established gardens and the mature grapevine that yielded a healthy harvest every year.

The artistry of the woodwork and masonry alone was no longer cost-effective in newer, suburban-style homes. They didn't have the charm or character of homes built in the 1940s and '50s. In our Minneapolis neighborhood, giant elms lined the boulevard on both sides, reaching towards each other to form a canopy over the street. The trees in the outlying areas were younger, rarely over twenty feet tall. They were sterile, uniform, and reeked of suburban conformity.

Dad did an excellent job finding our new home on the outskirts of the city. It was in the remaining blocks of houses before the city morphed into the suburbs. Mom could still shop where she had always shopped, and church was still within driving distance.

A much smaller, single-story rambler-style home was easier to keep up, and utility bills were manageable. Mom liked the fact that it had flower beds she could plant, and ample area for added gardening.

The move was made easier by the fact that my sister Joanne and her husband Don had bought our old home, and it was staying in our family. Mom was relieved by that and began looking forward to the new place, calling it her "dollhouse."

We moved in late spring. Most of my siblings were able to help with the move, and it was great having them around. Echoes of loud laughter from the house full of boxes and the now-empty truck faded quickly as everyone went their own way once again. I was feeling low now that things had quieted. It was back to the new realities of trying to get a grip on this drastically changed life.

The three of us did our best to adapt to the new surroundings. Spring happens late in Minnesota, so we still had time to get in the flower beds. Mom took care of those while Dad planted tomatoes. It was my job to cut the grass. As we worked together, we began to settle in and get a sense of home.

Mid-June arrived quickly. We lived amid boxes of clothing and household items. They would be taken care of as time allowed. I was still trying to adjust my lifestyle away from the "old friends" I needed to avoid, by order of the court. I had to limit contact with so many of the people I had known. The new neighborhood was without young people, and my co-workers on the new job went about their days in a zombie-like, catatonic state. Home to work, work to home.

I was bored and needed to connect with people my own age. My social life had come to a complete halt, and I felt isolated and alone. So many of my close friends had gotten in trouble as well, and were either spaced out on drugs or had been arrested, and I couldn't associate with them. Either way, it was tough to find friends to talk to.

Friday night came, and it was party time for most everyone my age. It was difficult to find friends who didn't drink, smoke weed, or both. I cashed my paycheck after work and stopped by to visit friends I was still allowed to be around. I had known most of them from the neighborhood, and they were good kids who liked to have a few beers when their work week was finished. I joined them for a cold beer but decided to leave when someone fired up a joint. Possession of even a small amount was still a felony, and I was uncomfortable with that.

"Hey, don't split yet, party's just getting started!" someone shouted.

"Thanks, but I have to head home."

"Home, really? It's Friday night, man!"

"Yeah, home, man!" I said sarcastically. "You guys know that I'm on probation. Risking jail time to smoke a joint isn't happening."

"Sorry, I forgot."

"Besides, my folks are going out of town early tomorrow and I want to spend time at home with them tonight," I said, setting my empty on the table.

"Out of town! Party's at your house tomorrow night, then?"

"Did you hear a *word* of what I just said? Damn, man, give me a break!"

All that was true, but I was also anticipating time at home in an empty house where I could find a small place in time to reconnect with my female identity. I had not found that opportunity in such a long time. I looked forward to unpacking boxes of clothing and finding things I had not tried on forever.

The longing to be myself would be satisfied, at least temporarily. There was not much to look forward to lately, and I was going to take advantage of this rare chance to express my hidden self, even if it was privately.

Dinner plates had been cleared from the table by the time I got home, but Mom pulled a plate of meatloaf from the warm oven for me.

"We'll be back Sunday night. I stocked the fridge with some sandwich meats, made a casserole you can heat up, and there's plenty of bread and milk."

"You didn't have to do all that, Mom; I'd be good with pizza delivery," I said jokingly.

"*Exactly* why I did it!"

She had rebounded well from the anguish I had caused last year with my arrest, but giving up her home, closing the family business, and dad having less income were all challenging for her. She somehow managed to keep her sense of humor and cope with life's abrupt changes.

Getting ready to go to bed, I emptied my pockets, including a wad of bills from my cashed paycheck, onto the top of the dresser.

Dad popped his head into my room. "Hang onto that money, kid, it's getting pretty damn hard to come by," he said, smiling a little, knowing firsthand the realities of that statement.

"Don't worry, I'm not going to blow it all in one place. Wake me before you guys leave if I'm not up already," I said.

Lying in bed, I was grateful for the love Mom and Dad had always shown me, but especially in recent times. I had been in such trouble a few months earlier, and in return, they showed nothing but support and concern for my well-being. They never gave up on me, even as life became more difficult for them. I knew how fortunate I was to have their forgiveness and love.

Mom and Dad rarely had time off, as long as I could remember, and tomorrow's trip was not a vacation. They were going to visit my aunt, a retired nun who was very ill. They wanted one last visit before she passed away. Two of my cousins, much older than I, would be joining them and riding in the same car.

It was pre-dawn, and lights were on in the house. I hurried out of bed so I could say goodbye. I wanted to see them before they left. I could see my two cousins sitting in the car outside, waiting for my dad to load up while my mom finished getting ready. Mom stepped into the kitchen where I was standing.

"You have everything you need for the weekend?" she said, double-checking the fridge.

"Yeah, thanks," I said, still half-asleep.

Just then, Dad came up from behind, firmly grabbing my shoulders. "Take care of everything this weekend, we'll see you Sunday night."

We said our goodbyes, and they headed out the kitchen door to the waiting car.

As they got in the car, I waved to everyone as they drove off.

Back in the house, I was alone. Alone for the first time in a long while.

I began unpacking boxes of clothing to put away, and it was not long before I found some colorful dresses that I'd had on in the past, and other women's clothing that had come from the attic of our old house. Some were Mom's, some my sister's from long ago. I recognized one that was a gorgeous lace-covered long dress that I had wanted to try on, but never had the chance. I began trying them on. I had lost a lot of weight recently, and was pleased when I zipped up that first dress, and it fit.

I was instantly freed from the machine oil, the tedious work, the compliant probation. Everything crystallized in a few moments. I was myself, and I loved it.

I found some lipstick and blush in the bathroom cabinet and applied them with joy. I was savoring every moment and wanted it to last all weekend. I had pushed this part of myself down so deeply, but it always found its way back, like it had never been abandoned.

I happily continued trying different clothes and made myself useful by unpacking and putting things away in the process. I was energized and put it to good use.

Dawn had fully broken now, and the house filled with daylight. I was so involved; I was not sure how long I had been at this when the phone in the kitchen rang out like an alarm.

Startled and wondering who would be calling this early on a Saturday morning, I hurried to pick it up.

"This is the Minneapolis Tribune news desk calling," a voice said when I answered. "Who am I speaking with?"

"The newspaper? Is this a prank call?"

"No, is this Michael?"

How did he know my name? "Yes, what is this about?"

"I have to ask an important question, Michael."

"Go ahead."

"Was your mother one of the other victims in the car your father was killed in this morning?"

Stunned, I didn't respond. Had he just said my father was killed?

"What are you talking about?" I stammered.

I felt like I had hold of a 220-volt live wire as my heart dropped to the floor. I held the phone away from my ear.

"Michael, hello Michael," I heard his small voice through the air, from the receiver beside me.

I grabbed the phone and said shakily, "I don't have any idea what you are talking about. Why would you ask a question like that?"

He sounded aghast. "Oh my God, I am so sorry, haven't the state troopers arrived at your house?"

"State troopers? What state troopers?" I said.

"I am truly sorry for your loss; I had no idea no one had come to your house to notify you yet. The state troopers were supposed to have done that."

I was numb as it sank in that this was for real, and my mom and dad had been in a terrible accident.

"I am sorry," he said one more time as he hung up.

The adrenaline was pumping, and I'm not even sure how I got there, but I found myself in the basement where the boxes of clothing were. I quickly pulled off the clothes I had on and wiped the makeup off my face. "This can't be true, please let this not be happening," I thought.

Throwing on a T-shirt and jeans, I headed back upstairs just as the doorbell rang. I could see the State Troopers through the door's sidelight window. "No. God damn it. This IS really happening," I thought.

As I opened the door, the troopers removed their hats. "Are you Michael?"

"Yes"

"Can we come inside?"

"Yes, come in."

Hats in hand, they looked deeply serious.

"We have some terrible news for you, Michael. It's about your mother and father."

"I know. The Tribune reporter called me a few minutes ago." My stomach was churning now.

"The Tribune? They're not supposed to call family members until they have been informed," the other officer interjected. "I am so sorry you heard about it that way."

"The reporter mentioned other victims," I said, "what was he talking about?"

"This must be extremely difficult; would you like to sit down?" he said, motioning toward the sofa.

"No, I'll stand here."

I felt like my legs couldn't move, and my heart was beating so rapidly that my head throbbed.

"Let me start over. I did not expect you to have heard any of this," one officer said. "The vehicle your mother and father were traveling in was hit head-on at a high rate of speed by a drunk driver early this morning just outside of Hastings, Minnesota, on Highway 61."

I sat down in the chair in the hallway by the door, fearing I would fall. My legs had no strength.

He continued, "I am sorry to inform you that there were no survivors and a total of five victims. The driver of the other vehicle was a 21-year-old woman who had just left a bar, where she had been kept for several hours past closing time due to her inebriation."

"Drunk driver at 6:00 in the morning?"

"Yes, apparently she had not completely sobered."

I didn't respond to that. It was all too much to absorb. Dumbfounded, speechless, I sat silently. How could this happen?

One officer spoke, awakening me from my withdrawn state: "Are there other family members living in this house?"

"No, my brothers and sisters are all living elsewhere."

"Would you like us to inform them? I'm not sure who else has been notified," he asked.

"No, thank you, I will get hold of one of my brothers or sisters and find out who has been informed. I have no idea if the Tribune reporter called any of them, but somehow, he knew my name."

"Please let us know if we can be of any help. If you are driving to your brothers or sisters, please be careful, you are in a state of shock right now," he said very kindly.

I can't recall what I did next. Everything was blurred, and nothing seemed real. What I do remember is guilt. I blamed myself. I was ashamed of how I'd wanted time home alone to indulge in my lifelong desires, and now Mom and Dad would never be coming home. I thought my selfish behavior was the reason they were taken so brutally and quickly. I was in shock and irrational, but I wouldn't get past that guilt for a long time.

My gender issues now seemed trivial and meaningless. Why did I want to be female so badly that I couldn't leave it behind, no matter how many times I resolved to do so? I would try again.

For the time being, I didn't care about anything else in the world but being with my family.

Chapter Eight: Going South

I ripped another page off my yellow legal pad, crumpled it into a ball, and tossed it across the room. Preparing myself for an important job interview was proving to be a challenging task. I knew why I'd had so many different jobs over the last six years, but explaining the reasons to a potential employer was not an option. I needed to doctor my resume if I was going to get this job.

After my parents died, I'd once again grown detached and volatile. Though my sister Joanne and her husband Don had taken me in and treated me with love and respect, I needed to find a place of my own. I stayed only a month or so before I found an apartment and moved on. For the next five years, I bounced from job to job. I was unable to settle on a career path.

First, I attempted to run my own business as a licensed private investigator. My probation officer referred to this as the most amazing turnaround he had ever seen. He was impressed with my desire to be on the right side of the law, to the point of releasing me from probation and expunging my record with the courts so I could obtain my license. I would be hired to follow suspected cheating husbands or wives, locate runaway teens, stake out insurance fraudsters, and conduct surveillance on pilfering employees. This was interesting and exciting for a while, but it lacked steady cash flow, and eventually I had to realize it was not a business with a future, just a cool thing to do when you're twenty years old.

Next, I landed a trainee position with a national photographic company. I was traveling from one Sears store to another in the deep South, taking baby pictures while parents lined up throughout the store with their crying tots. It was my job to make them smile, then capture that precious moment on film. That was a tough assignment, considering I could barely force my own face to form a smile.

About three weeks into training, in the sweaty New Orleans humidity, a little blonde girl wouldn't stop screaming and threw every toy back at me that was intended to put a twinkle in her eyes. At the end of that day, I had had enough and quit. I did not consider the consequences. I had barely enough money to get home. Back in Minnesota, I was homeless and broke.

Desperate and frustrated, I could not envision a future of success or happiness. I wasn't aware of how hard I was working to suppress my gender identity; how I would not allow myself to feel genuine emotions out of fear that they might take me. I just knew I needed to make a change.

My oldest brother, Jerry, had once suggested I move down to Texas.

"Lots of opportunities for someone your age, and the weather is much better than up north. Call me if you decide to come down."

I didn't call him, but I threw everything I had in a car that was barely capable of the trip and hit the road. I wasn't even sure where I was headed when I left Minnesota. I only knew that I had to leave, and I pointed the car south.

A few days later, I found myself in Dallas. I checked into a cheap hotel and crashed for the night. I called Jerry the next morning.

"Mike! How the hell are you doing?"

"I'm good, Jerry. Remember a while back when you said I should think about coming to Texas?"

He was silent for a few seconds, as though he knew what I was going to say next. I could hear his kids yelling in the background and imagined he was chasing them off.

"Yeah, I do remember saying something like that. Are you coming this way?"

"Actually, I'm already here."

"You're here *now*?"

"Yeah, I'm in Dallas, close to the airport."

"No kidding! You're only about 25 minutes from my house. You have a place to stay?"

"Just this cheesy motel I stayed at last night, but I'll find something else as soon as I work a few days and get some cash in my pocket."

"Forget that! Write down these directions. You can stay at my house as long as you need."

Glancing around the room at the painted cinderblock walls and cheap décor, the decision was easy. "Thanks, Jerry, but just until I get on my feet."

The last time I had seen Jerry was at our parents' funeral. He had taken me aside and reassured me that he would be there if I needed help in any way. He was fifteen years older than I, and I didn't know him very well. I never had the chance to spend time with him because of our age difference... and the fact that he joined the Navy when I was five years old.

None of that mattered. When I arrived in Texas, we became close quickly. We shared many memories of our mom and dad, which helped us both through our loss. We were geographically far from the rest of our siblings, and that drew us closer together as well. He helped me get an entry-level job in hydraulic sales that offered educational training. It was highly specialized, technical, and offered job security in a large industry that had a shortage of technically trained professionals who understood the application of products.

I applied myself to it and stuck with the job long enough to get an education and experience, but inside, I still felt like something was missing. I moved into my own apartment quickly and continued to move from job to job, hoping to assuage my restlessness and unease.

Ultimately, I came across an ad for a sales position with a major brand of fashion lingerie that was based out of the Dallas Apparel Mart. Without thinking, I picked up the phone and luckily got the national sales manager's personal assistant on the line. I made enough of an impression to get an in-person interview that week.

Now here I was trying to fill the gaps in my employment history. I wasn't going to leave anything to chance. I would not let this slip through my fingers. I was still trying to find myself through my job, and this was getting me closer. I was desperate to connect with women through fashion, believing this would help me connect with my ignored self.

Seated at my desk, I pushed my chair back and tossed the legal pad I had been tearing up to the floor. Doctoring my resume was not the answer. That would only complicate things and was no way to begin a new career. I would be direct, honest, and sincere. If I laid it all out there and it was not good enough to get the job, then I needed to keep looking.

On the day of my interview, I dressed in my best blue suit and polished brown shoes, thinking how great it would be if I were able to wear a stylish, tailored woman's business suit. When I arrived at the Dallas Apparel Mart fifteen minutes early, I was directed to one of several security lines.

"Busy spot," I said to the security guard, handing him my identification.

"Yes, sir," the distinguished-looking older gentleman said, as he looked through his guest list. "It's market week, and it'll get pretty crazy around here. Job interview?"

"Yes, sir."

"Have you been here before?"

"No, first time."

"OK. It's easy to get lost in here, so follow my instructions and you'll be OK. Go straight through the atrium, then turn left and stay on that concourse for about three blocks, and it's on your right."

"Three blocks! Really, that far?"

"Yes, sir, and good luck."

Making my way toward the great hall, I was captivated by what I saw. It was as though I had just passed through the turnstile at Disney's Magic Kingdom. There was vibrant activity everywhere I turned. Smartly dressed women rolled racks of beautiful satin evening gowns into their showrooms while others decorated the showroom window displays. Not yet made-up models hurried into the back of the showroom with their make-up bags and scurried to get dressed on time. It was fast-paced, inspiring, and chaotic all at once. I was taking in every moment.

As I passed through the great hall atrium, I was intrigued by the large stage with a runway that extended far out into the audience seating area. This was where fashion shows played out for buyers, sellers, and the attending fashion press. At that moment, I knew I belonged here and had to become a part of this.

In the showroom, I found Mac Weintraub, the national sales manager from the New York home office. He was as New York as they come: abrupt and to the point, he didn't hesitate to tell you exactly what he thought, and as we shook hands, I felt my anxiety rise.

"You seem a little uncomfortable," Mac stated, as we sat so he could review my resume. "Are you OK?"

"I'm OK, just a little over-excited seeing all of this for the first time." My eyes were still shifting around the room as I tried to regain control.

"Understandable, but do you have trouble looking people directly in the eyes when you talk to them? Because if you can't do that, you create suspicion. And sales is about confidence and trust."

I composed myself, realizing I would lose any chance I had at this job if I didn't recover quickly. "No, sir, not usually. I let my excitement get the best of me. I've been waiting for an opportunity in this business for some time, and I just needed to settle for a minute."

Straightening up in my chair, I rallied, looking him directly in the eyes now and speaking with certainty.

"I am aware of the importance of inspiring confidence in all of my customers. I have more of a low-key approach. I'm not a high-pressure salesman. I prefer to convey integrity, honesty, and the benefit of the product itself in a sales presentation."

Leaning back in his chair, Mac smiled now. "Nice recovery. I can see you have some potential."

Hearing that, I drew a deep breath and relaxed for the first time since entering the showroom.

"You have some solid sales training. The business you've been in is technical and very different from ours. This would be a dramatic change. Why are you interested in the women's apparel business?"

I swallowed hard, concealing my sudden panic attack. All my life, I'd been terrified of being exposed as a fraud, an imposter posing as a man, concealing the truth that inside I was a woman. I feared humiliation and ridicule. My mind always went back to the shame and teasing I encountered as a child when I dressed as a girl. Ironically, just moments before my interview, I had imagined what a wonderful life I could have living as a young woman with a career in this industry I so quickly fell in love with.

On the plus side, I'd developed a panic defense mechanism that helped me become a better salesperson. I learned to think on my feet and respond quickly to my emotions. I could turn a situation around and make it work in my favor. This is a technique that the best salespeople develop with years of experience. I had been perfecting it all my life.

I responded without hesitation.

"I am intrigued by the excitement. The vibrant atmosphere surrounding this market is unlike anything I've ever seen. It's interesting because it is constantly changing. I like the newness of fashion and the development of fresh designs every few months. It's just exciting. I like the challenge of finding new accounts and increasing existing customers' purchases as each new fashion season is presented."

Mac smiled, then concern flickered across his face. "So, why do you think you have the qualifications to succeed in this business?"

"I can apply the same fundamentals and sales habits I have established to any product that I am promoting. I plan my sales agenda, evaluate prospective accounts, and implement that strategy in whatever industry I'm in."

"Good, I like that attitude, but let me ask you why you have such a big gap in your resume from age 19 to 21. Did you travel the world, go to school, what?"

In anticipation of this question, I was prepared.

"Honestly, there was a lot of turmoil in my life then, and it can't be explained in a resume. I lost my parents in a car accident when I was 19, and was disconnected from what most people would consider a path in life that had structure or reasonable goals. I took time to get control of myself and realize the need to stabilize, and I did it eventually."

Mac looked concerned and shifted in his chair again. "That's honest, but should I be concerned about a relapse in behavior?"

"No. I kept myself employed all of that time, but wasn't grounded enough to keep my interest level up and didn't always make the best decisions. I did learn a lot through it all."

Mac studied my face, and I felt like he was looking through me.

"Let me be honest with you also. I am not looking for someone I'm going to have to replace in a few weeks or months. This is an entry-level job, but it's a career position in a very lucrative and rewarding business. You also need to know that the territory open is large geographically and will require you to travel to your customers 40 weeks a year, then be back in this showroom for markets five weeks a year, and in New York for market weeks. Are you prepared to be on the road that much?"

"Absolutely," I said enthusiastically.

"Great. If I hire you, you will be trained as all of our salespeople are, traveling with four different sales reps in four regions of the country, one week with each. Are you confident you can handle that?"

"Yes, sir. I'm not married, and travel is something I enjoy. I will commit 100 percent of my time to this and am self-motivated, so I can work well on my own. I look forward to training in the different regions, too."

I felt like bursting inside. It sounded like he was going to offer me this job in this one interview.

"I like what I've heard today, and I go by my instincts. I have a good feeling about you and am going to take a chance on you. When can you start training?"

I almost fell off my chair. "As soon as you need me."

"Wonderful. I believe you can be successful with us. I have been interviewing all week, and you clearly are what I am looking for. I appreciate your honesty, and I like the fact that you have a serious business background. You would be surprised how many candidates have no sales or business experience who think this is a whimsical business that's easy and fun. It can be fun, but it's not easy. It is often ruthless and unpredictable. I don't think you will disappoint me."

Making sure I looked directly in his eyes, I reached across his desk and firmly shook his hand.

"Welcome aboard."

As I walked down the corridor, my feet barely touched the ground. I was over the moon. I had forgotten joy like this existed. I hadn't felt this since childhood. For the first time in my life, I'd taken a job not because I was desperate or settling, but because it was what I wanted, and made me feel good about who I was inside. This would not be work; it would be a labor of love. It changed my entire outlook on life.

Chapter Nine:
Same Story, New Direction

I set the last suitcase in the trunk of my beat-up Oldsmobile Delta 88 and dusted off my hands.

I was starting over with nothing but an aging car that might not make the trip. This time I'd be traveling north on the same highway that had taken me to Texas ten years ago. I was saddened to leave behind a business I had loved and identified with.

Over those years, that first entry-level job had led to more: developing my own independent sales rep business representing several fashion lines. I had my own showroom in the Dallas Apparel Mart, and I worked with principal owners of fashion houses and retail store buyers. I attended fashion weeks in New York and Los Angeles. My career has allowed me to live my gender identity without forcing me to directly confront it. I thought of myself as a successful businesswoman who couldn't convey that outwardly but who was deeply in touch with herself through the business of women's fashion.

Showing my lines of dresses, separates, suits, bridal, and formal wear to my customers became my passion. Each time I presented new fashions to buyers, I shared their excitement as they reacted to a piece they thought was beautiful, while I felt we were connecting on a deeper personal level as women. I could work twelve hours a day and not realize that time had gone by.

I'd receive new sample lines five times a year, and each time it was like Christmas morning, opening the boxes and revealing the excitement of the new season's offerings to show my clients. I could not imagine ever leaving this dream. It was a consolation prize for my soul. Maybe I could never actually become a woman, but I was living it through my work and relationships.

But Mac Weintraub was right. This business was cutthroat. As retail began to change, things became treacherous. Some companies I represented accepted my orders but didn't pay my commissions; more established reps cannibalized smaller reps' product lines, putting them out of business. I fought for my livelihood as long as I could, but it became untenable. I had to give up.

Coming to that conclusion was not easy. I'd put up everything I had to keep the business going. I depleted my savings account, gave up my apartment, sold my car for cash, and bought a junker so I could pocket the difference and have money to live on. I was approaching the familiar territory of financial disaster, but that wasn't the worst of it.

A year before everything fell apart, I began a relationship with a woman I'd met at a diner I frequented. I asked her out for a drink the night we met, and we ended up in bed. From there, it became an anytime, anywhere, sexual infatuation for us. Outside of the bedroom, I was taken by her fun-loving personality, and talk turned to our mutual future. Maybe I could lead a 'normal life' after all, and have a family with children.

Unfortunately, from the minute my financial troubles began, she became distant, only returning my calls when she felt the need for sex. She judged me, telling me I didn't have the ambition to succeed, and she needed someone who was a 'go-getter.' I was deeply hurt by her barbs. I'd put my heart and soul into my work and expected support from the woman I'd begun to trust.

Abruptly, I ended things with her. Once the sting faded, I began to realize much of our connection had been based on sexual attraction, not love. I didn't see the signs, because this was a new game that I had not played. I'd spent years focused on my business, and because of my lack of steady experience with women, I misinterpreted our sexual chemistry. This had been lust, not love. What else was I not seeing clearly? I needed to make drastic changes in all aspects of my life.

Discouraged yet hopeful, I decided I needed a complete change in surroundings to forget what I was leaving behind. I had been missing my family in Minnesota and the natural beauty of the state I grew up in. It would be good for my soul to return to the place I left when I was barely 21, struggling, and in an awful emotional state.

Now, I closed the trunk and slid into the driver's seat. I'd hit rock bottom so many times. It was a familiar place where I understood how to find my way out. What would one more time hurt?

After arriving in Minnesota, I swallowed my pride and took a job selling novelty comic-strip character sweatshirts and T-shirts over the phone. It was a long, hard fall from being a multi-line independent sales rep in Dallas. I went from the excitement of fashion weeks and models to telephone soliciting in a sweatshop in the warehouse district of Minneapolis. But I kept my hopes high and remained positive that a new beginning was on the horizon.

I knew this work was necessary and temporary. It allowed me to save enough to rent an apartment. In my off hours, I spent all my free time searching for a better opportunity.

It only took about a month before I spotted an ad in the Minneapolis newspaper for a salesman at a distribution company of hydraulic products. I was excited to see that their main product line was one I was very familiar with, as it was the same brand of technical products I had trained on and sold when I had been in that business in Texas.

I spent hours researching materials and familiarizing myself with their current technologies.

I was confident and prepared and landed the job on my first interview. A few weeks later, I was helping a friend paint his house. It had been a typical muggy Minnesota summer day when the last place you wanted to be was working outside. I had the grueling task of scraping the old paint off the eaves on the underside of the roof. Up on a ladder, sweating profusely and weary of the tedium, I heard a voice from below.

"Get down here and take a break, I've got lunch."

Wiping the sweat off my brow, I turned my eyes downward. Who was this woman inviting me down for lunch? Must be a friend of Hal's fiancée, I thought.

"Sounds great, be right down." I had two good reasons to stop working: lunch and to meet this great-looking woman.

Everyone headed to the kitchen, and she followed with a very large bucket of Kentucky Fried Chicken. It turned out her name was Trish, and she did in fact work with Hal's fiancée, Nancy, in managed care at an insurance company. As we exchanged introductions, I noticed she was wearing a T-shirt from Rick Newman's Catch a Rising Star comedy club in New York City.

"Love the T-shirt," I said, grabbing a drumstick. "Have you been to New York recently?"

"Yes, I just got back a few days ago. The son of a good friend of mine manages comedians in New York, and we went to some of the shows. I love the city." She took a seat across from me at Hal's kitchen table.

"Me too. I love comedians... except when they bomb on stage, though, that's very uncomfortable."

We connected instantly. Later, I would joke with her, "Baby, you had me at Kentucky Fried."

Within a few weeks, I called her, and we went out for dinner at a nice Italian restaurant in downtown Minneapolis.

"So, did you grow up in Minnesota?" I asked after we'd ordered dessert.

"No, I moved here from Kansas City about fourteen years ago," she replied.

I pushed my chair away from the table, allowing my full stomach more room. "Wow, I guess that qualifies you as a real Minnesotan, except I haven't heard you say yah, you betchya, or okie dokie then!"

Trish shifted in her chair, leaning back to relax. "Well, I was wondering the same thing. You moved here from Texas, and I don't hear the twang in your voice — you haven't said 'y'all' once!"

"Hah! That's because I worked hard to keep my northern accent. I've seen too many Yankees move to Texas, buy huge cowboy hats, and talk like they were raised on a cattle ranch."

"Well, thank God for that. What brought you back here?" Trish asked.

I hesitated for a few moments, unsure how much I was ready to reveal about the devastation that compelled my return. Would she think of me as a weak man, or would I be exposing my feminine self if I confessed my misery and emotional distress? But I wanted an honest, open relationship from the start, so I poured my heart out.

There was something I trusted in her. I had no trouble opening up. "Long story short, I was in an intensely passionate relationship that I mistook for love. I was being used for sex only, which is not a bad thing if that's all you are looking for. But I was convinced this was the real thing... and she saw things differently. Before it ended, she showed her true self, and I didn't see it coming. I was hurt and needed a fresh start. Plus, my business tanked, and I figured if I had to start over, I should come back home to Minnesota."

Trish put her elbows on the table and leaned in closer. "I'm really sorry to hear that. Nobody should be treated that way. But this is really amazing!"

Amazing in a good or bad way? I thought.

"How so?" I asked.

I motioned to the server for the check while Trish began to elaborate.

"I just broke up with a guy who put me through the same wringer. I was sure our lives were going somewhere together, but he kept stringing me along, just for the sex. There was no hope of any real relationship," Trish said.

I was relieved by her reply. She understood where I was coming from. We'd shared our vulnerability.

"That is an astonishing coincidence. The timing of our meeting is impeccable!" I said.

Trish smiled. "Is this divine providence?"

Taking the opportunity to lighten things up, I replied, "No, it's just downtown Minneapolis."

Trish laughed. "Oh my God, and you're funny too. I love it."

We continued our true confessions. "I'll have to admit that was a once-in-a-lifetime type of relationship for me. I haven't had multiple dalliances in my time, maybe a one-off here and there," I said.

Trish began shaking her head. "I cannot believe the things we have in common. I'm the same way. I'm starting to think you can read my mind."

I decided to take the subject further. "We seem to have similar luck finding the real deal. It's not as if I'm a difficult person to be with, but I have dated a number of women in the last ten years who weren't right for me, the last being the most serious."

Trish gathered her thoughts for a minute while finishing her drink. "Well, once again, me too, except the last guy wasn't the one I thought was the love of my life. It was the one before him. I was sure of it, but it wasn't physical. He was kind and sensitive, funny and smart, like you. He had all of the traits I was looking for, except one."

I wondered what could be missing. "Sounds like a great guy. Can I ask what he didn't have?" I said.

Trish didn't hesitate. "Yes, a sexual attraction to women. We dated a long time before he came out as gay. I was crushed, and I cried for days. I was deeply in love with him."

I was startled by her revelation. Except for the part about not being attracted to women and being gay, she'd just described me. I didn't know how to react, so I just said,

"That must have been really difficult for you. What became of him after that?"

"I had feelings for him for a long time, but now I consider him a great friend."

I'd never had such a revealing conversation on a first date. We'd both trusted each other with our frailties; we'd both taken a chance with details about previous lovers that couples usually don't discuss for a while, if ever.

When I dropped Trish off at her place later, we gave each other a peck on the cheek.

"I hope I'm not the first person you're dating since your heartbreak," Trish said. "The one on the rebound never has a chance."

Still thinking about how well the night had gone, I said, "Don't worry. You're not – and I left it all behind in Texas. I am way over it."

Trish smiled, "Good! Me too. I think we should do this again soon."

"Great," I said. "Then I won't have to grovel for a second date."

Trish laughed, "Hey, I didn't say that!"

On my way home, I was still thinking about her boyfriend, who came out while dating her. The fact that she spoke highly of him, and they were still friends after an abrupt breakup, spoke volumes about the kind of person she was. She indicated her love for sensitive, tender men. That was encouraging. I wouldn't have to put up a macho front, as I'd done with my last girlfriend. I could simply be myself. Well, maybe not my *full* self. I sensed something very strong between us, and I wasn't going to let this gender demon get in my way. It would have to take the backseat on this trip. It had kept me from so many other things in my life, and I wasn't going to let it control me. I liked Trish and wanted to see her again.

After a few more dates, we talked as if we'd known each other for years, finishing each other's sentences and sharing similar opinions. Soon, I'd moved out of my rental and in with Trish. A few months later, we moved into a larger townhome we picked out together.

We shared interests in travel, theater, restaurants, and live shows. We both loved New York, so that was our first trip together. We took in some Broadway shows and did it on a tight budget. I joked about how tiny our room in the theater district was. I remember picking up the phone in the room and in my best Groucho Marx voice saying, "Hello, room service? Send up a bigger room."

We also discovered we could laugh at ourselves, even when we got testy with each other. On that trip to New York, it was record cold, with temperatures reaching 20 below zero. We were standing outside, unable to agree on where to go for dinner.

Freezing and tired of my indecision, Trish dramatically made her exit from the scene: "Well, I'm going back to the room. When you decide what you want to do, you come back up." She said this defiantly, like a starlet in some old Hollywood film.

"OK, fine. If that's what you need to do, go ahead," I said, frustrated with her.

I walked around outside by myself in the freezing cold, mumbling cuss words like an idiot until I was too cold to stay outside.

I went up to our room, knocked on the door, and waited for her to respond.

"What?" she shouted at me.

"Well!" I said, mimicking her flaming delivery, "When you're ready to come out of that room and have dinner, you let me know!"

After a silence, she opened the door, looked at me seriously, then started laughing, and I joined in. This humorous approach to disagreements would be a valuable tool in keeping the lines of communication open between us in tough times.

The week after our trip, when Trish went back to work, Nancy told her she had been diagnosed with breast cancer, and it was very aggressive. It was devastating news to us, but particularly for Trish. Nancy was her best friend.

We had no idea how quickly the cancer would spread, and spent as much time as we could with Nancy. The days became more difficult as the cancer advanced. She would go out to eat with us in her wheelchair and did her best to enjoy time with her friends, but it destroyed her body so rapidly that she went into home hospice care within a few months.

The November evening on which Nancy passed was cold and grey. The air was still, without a hint of a breeze. Afterward, Trish and I stood outside their home in an alcove, holding each other.

Nancy had several long, cylindrical wind chimes hanging in a corner where not much wind could ring them. As we stood quietly, a sudden gust sent the chimes into a loud frenzy. Puzzled, I looked at Trish.

She gazed back at me. "That was Nancy. I told her to give me a sign that she was OK when she left. That was her."

It was a surreal moment that we both wanted to believe in. Tears came to our eyes.

"That's why I love you, right there, Trish," I said. "You are such a beautiful soul."

In Trish, I found someone who stayed and gave love when times were the most difficult. She was so unlike my girlfriend in Texas, who thought only of herself and the easy way out.

Trish later revealed to me that our initial meeting had been set up by Nancy while I was helping paint the house.

"You've got to come and meet this guy," she told Trish. "You're perfect for each other."

Trish and I married the following May. This time it was authentic, a love worth waiting for.

Chapter Ten:
The Return of the Passenger

A year or so passed, and Trish and I settled into our shared life. We had successful careers, lots of close friends, family, and a house in a nice community. We did not have children, even though we tried everything possible with doctors and the technology that was available. It just was not meant to be.

We were disappointed but had a mutual understanding that our love was not based on our ability to reproduce. We accepted that and moved on.

When you find the love of your life later than most people, you have great reverence and appreciation for each other. It's crystal clear what you've found when you have lived so long without it.

But even in the best times of my life, I could not escape my deepest truth. I knew what was in my heart. I couldn't fully define it, but it was always there. My struggle with gender identity was not about to let go, however hard I tried to loosen its grip.

Still, I refused to let this inner self destroy the love I had for Trish or interrupt the life we shared. I believed that in order for our relationship to continue to prosper, I had to continue to repress what was inside of me. I was a good jailkeeper, proficient at imprisoning myself, using fear and conscience for steel and concrete.

I focused on my commitment to Trish and the promise I'd made to be her husband. We were not deeply religious, but were both believers who attended church most Sundays. Raised Catholic, I understood guilt and knew how to impose it upon myself. It was a useful weapon in my prison guard arsenal. I believed that if I were to reveal my feelings to Trish, it would be a selfish act of a fool...but deep-seated feelings have a way of escaping captivity.

The escape plan began to form one evening as Trish thumbed through the mail.

"Hey," she said, "we got an invitation to a Halloween costume party at Val's house. I haven't been to a costume party in ages."

On the couch, I continued to flip channels on the TV. My ears perked up. I hadn't dressed up for Halloween since I was a kid.

"Could be fun," I said. "What would we go as?" I knew exactly what I wanted to do with this opportunity, but I waited to see what Trish would suggest.

"I hadn't thought about it." Trish joined me on the couch.

"Maybe a couple's costume?" I said, pausing my channel surfing on *Wheel of Fortune*. "We could go as the Wheel of Fortune and Vanna White!" I exclaimed.

"You know what would be funny?" Trish scrutinized the picture on TV. "YOU be Vanna and I'll be the wheel!"

My mind immediately went back to childhood memories of Halloween. I thought of how, when I was twelve, my mom had suggested I go out as a girl. Over the years, I'd played back that moment. I thought I was so clever, somehow getting her to suggest it, but in reality, she knew what I wanted.

I got off the couch and walked over to the TV.

"That would be hilarious, and the costumes would be easy to make."

Trish looked at the screen once again. "Sure, you were in the dress business. You won't have any trouble picking out something pretty, but I'll have to make a wheel."

"You're crafty, you'll come up with something clever in no time," I said.

I was taken by the fact that she suggested this so quickly. Was it similar to what my mom had done? Trish knew me so well. Did she sense that I would enjoy this costume idea?

Wouldn't it be fantastic if I could share this with Trish now? Maybe not just yet, I thought.

We had a few weeks to prepare our costumes. I was obsessed with finding the right dress, hair, shoes, and makeup. I found a prom dress at a bridal shop that was perfect for the role of Vanna. It was a long, form-fitting purple satin with a thigh-high split up one side. They also had larger-sized shoes that matched the outfit, and some costume jewelry for special occasions.

When I showed Trish what I had put together, she was surprised. "Wow, you are really getting into this, aren't you?"

"Yeah. I suppose so. It's a fun idea, and if I'm doing this, I'm going to look good." I underplayed my excitement, same as always. I didn't want to expose my real desire to dress femininely.

She showed me the wheel of fortune she'd made from a large round platter, aluminum foil, and different colored triangles cut from crepe paper, hanging from suspenders she would wear.

I moved in close to her and said slyly, "Put your wheel on, honey. I'll take you for a spin."

The anticipation was almost too much, and when Halloween night finally arrived, I couldn't wait to get my costume on and see what it felt like to set free the inner woman whom I'd held prisoner through my entire adult life. The excitement escalated as I dressed. Trish helped with my makeup and the finishing touches.

Stepping out into the brisk evening air in a beautiful dress, wig, and makeup felt like walking into a dream. I was overwhelmed by a sense of congruence — I finally felt *right* with myself.

On this night, I would allow my hidden self to be expressed outwardly, knowing I would turn into a pumpkin at midnight.

We had a wonderful time at the party. I was playfully teased by the guys and flattered when our women friends told me how good I looked. That reinforced my sense of well-being. I allowed my instincts to take over and played the role well. Who would know that I wasn't really playing at all? This was me, being myself under the cover of a costume.

Once we were back home, I was struck by the similarities between how I felt when I was a child and how I feel now. I did NOT want this night to end, and I did NOT want to take my costume off. Why couldn't this last forever? I was so secure in how I felt as a woman and so certain I didn't want to go back to 'normal'.

Trish and I 'spun the wheel' several times before I was finally ready to call it a night.

"You really loved doing this, didn't you?" Trish said as we lay in bed afterward.

"Sex, absolutely!"

"No, not just that, you know what I mean. You loved dressing up and going out. I could see how much you were enjoying yourself."

Startled, I wasn't sure how to answer, but I was as honest about that night as I could be. I rolled to face her, propping my head up on my arm.

"Yes, I really did enjoy myself. It reminded me of Halloween when I was a kid. My mom let me dress as a girl, and I loved it."

"Really? Then we should do this more often."

"I'd like that a lot."

Rolling over, closing my eyes, I was content. I could never reveal myself to the world, but if I knew I had these moments to look forward to, I'd be able to get through my life. Or so I thought.

The next Halloween, we went to a costume party at a bar/restaurant that offered live music and dancing. I was more daring this time, in a long, sleek black dress with a high slit up one leg.

We were enjoying the music and a drink when a young Latino man came over to our table and asked me to dance.

Startled, I said, "No thanks, I'm with someone," and I continued talking with Trish. He shrugged and went back to his table.

Trish laughed that this guy was hitting on me. "See how it feels to be pursued? I think he likes you."

I knew I wasn't attracted to men, but it felt good to be asked. It meant he saw me the way I understood myself. Still, it was a new situation. I hoped he wasn't offended by my refusal.

"Trish, I think he's staring at me."

"Ha-ha, you're right. I think he's in love!"

Before I could say anything else, the man got out of his chair and started back our way.

Standing closer to our table, he bent over towards me and very sincerely asked again, "Just one dance, please! It won't be so bad."

"I'm sorry if you misunderstood. This is a Halloween party, and this is my costume," I said as I pulled on my shoulder strap.

"You don't like me, it's OK, but I am a really nice guy," he replied.

I realized I was analyzing his expression and body language for clues as to whether I was safe.

He looked disappointed, not angry, so I blurted out, "No, really, I'm in a costume and I am a man."

He looked confused, but for the wrong reasons. "You are mad? Why are you mad at me? I'm sorry to make you mad, but I only wanted to dance."

Trish was doing all she could to stifle her laughter.

"I'm sorry for the misunderstanding. I said I am a MAN—not MAD."

Still not getting what I was trying to tell him, he said, "Sorry I made you so mad," and slowly walked back to his chair.

Trish was still laughing, "I'm not sure he understood anything you just said, but I'm sure you broke his heart."

"He must really be wasted," I said.

"The language barrier didn't help matters," Trish replied.

"Let's finish our drinks and go home. I mean, how drunk do you have to be to mistake me for a woman, even after you hear my voice?"

I couldn't let Trish see how good this had made me feel. Inside, my heart raced, knowing that a man was attracted to me as a woman, so I had to write it off to him being drunk.

On the way home, we decided to be more selective about Halloween destinations. Even though I'd felt validated by the man's unrelenting advances, I knew men who felt misled could be dangerous. In the future, we'd stick with costume parties.

The next year, we went to an event in Las Vegas billed as the "world's largest Halloween and fantasy festival," where "all of your dreams come true." It was impressively organized. Guests with pre-paid tickets were greeted with complimentary cocktails, and everyone seemed eager to strut their stuff.

There were lots of drag queens, many dressed in thigh-high boots, short skirts, and goth makeup. As Trish and I sipped cocktails, I sensed a theme developing.

"Is it just my imagination, Trish, or are most people in black leather and vinyl?" I gazed down at my blue gingham Dorothy dress.

"Nope, you're not imagining that. Skin-tight leather!" Beside me, Trish wore a scarecrow costume.

"Did we miss something when we read the itinerary?"

Trish gazed around the room. "Yeah, I'm thinking we did."

"Oh well, we're here and it's paid for, let's check it out."

We grabbed our drinks and started taking in the crowd and the different rooms. Everyone seemed to take our tame costumes in stride.

We received lots of compliments on our costumes, each time replying, "Thanks, and yours is great too."

When we got out of earshot, we joked about it: "And I *love* the leather mask. Just where do I get one with chains on it like that?"

We threaded our way through the wide hallways of the convention center, passing people taking photographs, chatting, and complimenting each other's costumes. We paused outside of one room whose occupants overflowed into the hallway.

"Must be something interesting going on in there," Trish said. "Everyone wants in."

Entering, it was hard to see or hear. The room was flooded with red light, highlighted by ultraviolet laser beams shooting across the ceiling. The music was a loud, pulsating club beat. Bodies seemed to be moving all around us as we moved towards the main stage.

Trish and I stood in amazement. Onstage, a dominatrix stood wearing a vinyl catsuit, whips and all. She was administering spankings to each person as they got their turn. She was flanked left and right by two henchmen who were clad in ominous hooded leather outfits. They stood guard with arms folded, staring into the crowd for effect. They occasionally grabbed random victims and put them in restraints, adding to the drama.

"Do you suppose they pay extra for that?" I said in amazement.

"We are definitely NOT in Kansas anymore!" Trish gasped.

"I'm not even sure what planet we're on," I said.

We continued making Oz jokes to lessen the shock.

"I can always click my heels together and we can get the hell out of here."

"I don't think that's how it works, but try closing your eyes and repeating 'there's no place like home' three times," Trish replied.

"Nope, still here, Trish. On the bright side, we're not overdressed. I mean, look at us, could we be more out of place in our innocent little costumes?"

Laughing again, Trish said, "I think I did see some normal costumes a while back. A few Frankensteins and mummies. They must not have gotten the memo either."

"Hah. Or maybe it's just one of those S&M black-leather-optional parties."

"Are you sure you don't want to get in line for this?" Trish joked.

"Well, I have been naughty, but I think I'll pass this time."

Not being ones to judge others for their entertainment preferences, we sat down across from another couple at an open table. "Interesting room, isn't it?" Trish said to the woman who wore a black witch costume.

"Wonderful, my husband and I love this. We come every year," she said.

Her husband, in an executioner-looking outfit, leaned towards me.

"We're from Iowa, we don't get many opportunities to participate in events like this."

"I can see that. What do you do back home? "I asked.

"I'm an accountant."

"Great escape then, right?"

"My favorite night of the year."

As much as this was not our thing, we understood that everyone was there for the same basic reason: escaping reality and having fun. Extreme for our taste, but it was what they enjoyed, so who were we to judge them?

We finished our drinks and walked back to our hotel.

"Let's cross this one off the list." Trish sounded adamant.

"Yep, I don't feel quite at home with that crowd either," I replied.

"I wouldn't think so. How do we keep getting into these situations on Halloween?" Trish asked.

"Guess we need to find a better outlet for my dressing up."

We stepped off the main strip, into a quiet little bar for a nightcap and to chat. I was happy, I was still 'in character'.

Very thoughtfully, Trish took my hand. "Maybe this whole Halloween thing isn't the answer."

"Meaning what?"

Then she totally caught me off guard. "Well, I'm pretty sure that the reason we do this 'Halloween thing'" Trish made air quotes with her fingers, "is because you're able to express yourself openly as a woman. Do you think maybe there's more to this?"

I wasn't sure exactly what she meant. "More to it in what way?"

"I don't know. I just see how happy you are when you're dressed up. You seem like a different person. Do you think you might want to be a woman?"

My heart raced as I thought about that possibility and my reply. How certain was I about myself? How damaging could my honesty be? I knew how I felt, but did I truly know why?

Holding her hand tighter, I looked down at the table and back up into her eyes again a few times. "The reality is, Trish, I don't know for sure. What you've noticed is very real. I do feel at my best when I'm dressed as a woman. I feel very natural. I can't say that I understand why, but I've always felt this way."

More deeply concerned now, she leaned back in her chair and thought for a moment.

"So, where do we go from here to find out more?" Trish asked.

"I don't know. Therapy isn't really in our budget."

"That's for sure, but we just can't leave this hanging." She exhaled loudly as she spoke.

I thought about it silently for a moment, then recalled something I'd recently read.

"Here's a thought. The University of Minnesota has a reputation for being at the forefront of gender studies. Maybe they have a free help program or can at least recommend someone affordable that can offer some direction."

"That's a possibility worth looking into," she said, relaxing a little now.

"Yeah, maybe I can find someone who can figure out what's been going on in this head of mine for so long."

Trish smiled. "Good luck with that part."

The conversation shifted to other topics, and I wondered if I should have just said no to her question about being a woman. It would have been the easy answer, but I did need help figuring myself out, and I wasn't going to slam the door shut now that Trish had opened it.

The next Monday, I called the University of Minnesota and briefly explained my gender identity issues. They didn't seem prepared for my questions, mentioning that this program was relatively new and understaffed. They said they would transfer me to the Department for Gender Studies, and someone could help me.

I waited a long time before a woman picked up the line. She didn't seem to have much knowledge about the program either.

"I can refer you to Melissa," she said.

"Melissa?" I repeated, reaching for a pen. "Is she a professor?"

"She doesn't work for the university," the woman said. "We refer these sorts of inquiries to her."

I wrote down Melissa's phone number, but the scrap of paper remained on my desk for two days before I got up the nerve to call.

"May I speak to Melissa?" I asked when a man answered.

"This is her; how can I help you?"

I wasn't sure if I understood. "You are Melissa?" I asked.

"Yes, who am I speaking with?"

Unsure if I wanted to continue the conversation, I hesitated.

"My name is Mike, and I got your name and number from the University of Minnesota. I had called them seeking information on their Gender Dysphoria program, and they sent me to you."

Melissa seemed surprised and pleased, which indicated she didn't get many referrals. "Great, what can I do to help?"

"I'm not sure. I'd like to speak with someone who is knowledgeable on the subject and who could help me out," I said.

"I have a lot of personal experience, and the University sends people who are interested in learning more about themselves my way, so you've come to the right place," she said.

"I'm not sure that could be done in a phone conversation." I wasn't ready to share personal information without meeting in person and getting a good idea of who I was dealing with.

"I agree. Can we meet in person?" she said.
I was curious to learn more. What did I have to lose?

"I'd like to bring my wife along. She's as much a part of this as I am."

"Wonderful! I can bring my wife too. When we meet, you can call me by my given name, Tom."

Not fully convinced this was for me, I stood silent for a moment. "OK, I think we should meet somewhere neutral...like a shopping mall."

"Sounds perfect," Melissa replied.

When the day arrived, Trish and I sat in the car for a few extra minutes. We didn't want to arrive first, so we could keep walking if things didn't look right.

Approaching the food court, Trish squeezed my hand as we headed towards the only couple standing apart from the crowd. They were glancing around, as people often do when waiting for someone they haven't met.

"You must be Mike and Trish," Tom said when he caught sight of us.

"That's us," I replied.

We grabbed a few of the cheap plastic chairs scattered around the food court. For some reason, Tom, Trish, and I ended up at one table, while Tom's wife sat alone at another.

"First, I'd like to ask you a few questions, Tom," I said, glancing at his wife, who looked uncomfortable.

"I didn't get any real background from the University on your qualifications. I don't mean to be rude, but do you have any education or training in gender studies?" I said.

Tom's eyes widened as if no one had asked him that before. He had a 'how dare you question the authority vested in me by the University of Minnesota' look.

Trish squeezed my hand under the table, signaling her discomfort.

"Well, not formally," he said finally. "I am involved in group therapy, in a sense."

At the other table, Tom's wife exhaled loudly. She didn't seem to approve of this meeting — or of Tom getting involved in other people's business.

"Oh, in a sense. What exactly does that involve?" I asked.

"I head up a local club that is part of a national organization." He said that with authority, perhaps hoping it would lend credibility to his status as a counselor.

"A club? What kind of club is that?" I asked.

I was surprised and dismayed to learn that Tom's only qualification was being president of a local chapter of a crossdressers club, a group of men who met monthly. He went on to explain that they dressed as women for these events only, then went back to their happy lives at home and work. The purpose was to share their experiences and support each other in their lifestyle. It became clear quickly that Tom's experiences were not mine.

"So, are there any guest speakers or discussions about gender identity?" I asked.

"Not specifically. We just have a good time and enjoy ourselves privately in a safe environment. It's more of a social gathering than anything else." Tom replied.

Great! I thought to myself, a lateral move to a bigger closet is just what I need.

Trish and I looked at each other.

"Well, I'm glad you have that, but that's not something I can see us getting involved in," Trish said.

"I respect what you're saying, but I think if you gave it a chance, you'd enjoy our club," Tom said.

Was he recruiting? Was that the point of this whole wasted evening? He offered no insight into where I might find REAL help. And his wife! Why did she even bother coming? Maybe she did us a favor, sitting in the background looking embarrassed to be there while her husband carried on about something she didn't seem to support.

"Sure, why not?" I said, knowing this would be the end of it.

We shook hands and parted ways. Trish and I took a walk around the mall to absorb what had just happened.

"Why in the hell did the University put me in touch with him? President of the Crossdressers Club? Really? What qualifies him to give expert advice on gender?"

I was upset. I thought I was getting professional, psychological help towards finding out who I was, and the University person pawned me off on someone with zero education in gender analysis.

Trish was still surprised by the events that had unfolded. "I had no idea clubs like that exist. I don't have a clue why the U of M refers people to them," Trish said as we walked.

"I didn't either. It strikes me as being like the group we ended up with in Las Vegas. The difference being, the Vegas group was into the S&M scene. Both groups meet in private and have their own form of self-expression. There's nothing wrong with that on its own, but it wouldn't answer any of my questions about why I feel the way I do."

After those words came out of my mouth, I realized there had been some benefit to this meeting with Tom/Melissa. It was now clear that something much deeper was going on than simply a desire to 'dress up.' I resented the assumption that I could resolve my problems by getting together with a group of men whose interests were limited to dressing up in private as a group, never resolving any deeper issues they may or may not have. I'm sure there are groups that meet who are interested in more, but this one wasn't described as one. I wanted clarity, and it was becoming clear that I thought of myself as a real woman, not a weekend warrior. Getting into the car, I slammed the door, still upset.

Trish held my hand as I started the car. "Hey, at least we've eliminated you joining any men's clubs as a solution."

We both had a good laugh at that, but reality sank in. Professional therapy would not be in our immediate future; we would keep going on as we were, for now.

The Uninvited Passenger

All five brothers together—oldest holding youngest (me).

Isabelle Tousignant

Contemplating life on my favorite stoop, popsicle in hand.
Dapper ring bearer, wishing for something else.

The Uninvited Passenger

With brother Richard—Mom dressed us alike, must've wanted twins. Pretending to catch brother Bill's swing and miss. Brother Bob teaching me to hold a bat bigger than myself.

Isabelle Tousignant

Mom and the "Final Four" kids—I'm out in front, of course.
Dad with the last five, including sister Mary Jane.

The Uninvited Passenger

My bandmates and me—our first paying gig. All eight of us with Mom and Dad at my brother's wedding—I'm having a bad hair day.

Isabelle Tousignant

All of my siblings together at Trish's and my wedding.
My three beautiful sisters, when they were all with us.

The Uninvited Passenger

Happily ever after—our wedding picture.
Honeymooning in Colorado.

Isabelle Tousignant

Pre-transition Halloween in Wilton Manors, Florida.

Trish and me on the north shore of Lake Superior. Us in Illinois at Christmastime, just before I revealed my truth to Trish.

Isabelle Tousignant

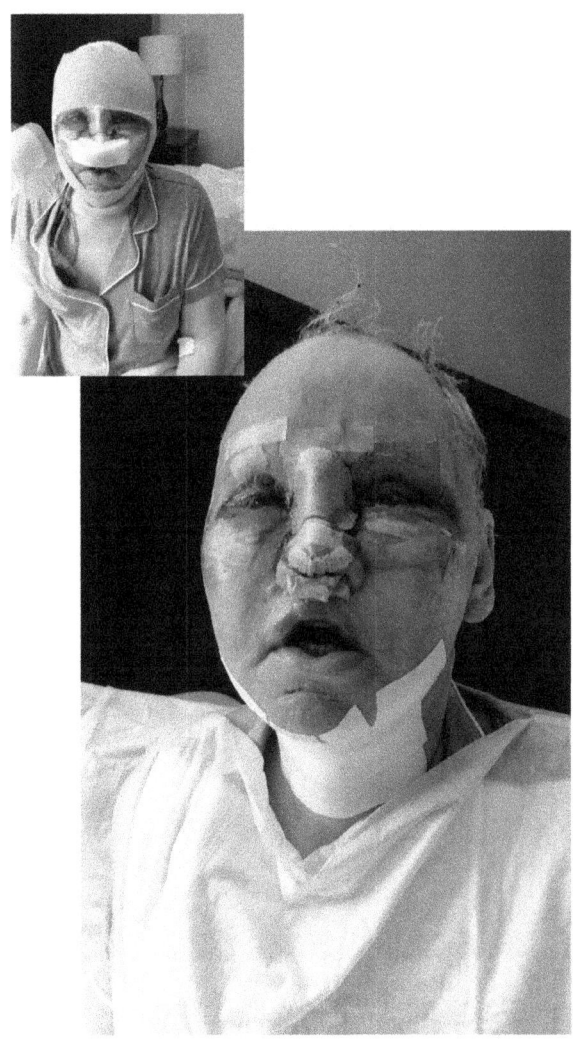

Recovering from eight-hour surgery—does this look whimsical?

The Uninvited Passenger

Six months later: joy, pure joy!

Florida outdoor gathering—Trish and me.

The Uninvited Passenger

Post-transition Halloweens in Florida.

Isabelle Tousignant

Our final Christmas in Florida—and happy to be home in Minnesota.

The Uninvited Passenger

Youth Outlook Services—charity event in Aurora, Illinois.

Chapter Eleven:
Minding Our Manors

The evolution of my understanding of myself may have been shelved for now, but the rest of our lives continued to move forward. Ten months after the meeting with Tom, we bought a timeshare on the beach in Fort Lauderdale. I had been in business for five years, and things were going great.

Steady growth and strong cash flow meant peace of mind and time to finally enjoy the benefits of success. Nearing the end of our first timeshare stay, we were in the lobby looking at the local papers for things to do. I came upon an ad that caught my eye immediately.

HAUNTED MANORS, WILTON MANORS, FLORIDA!

The greatest street festival/ Halloween celebration in South Florida!

Outdoor stages with live performers, street vendors with food and drinks.

Fantastic costumes and contests.

Costumes encouraged, but not required. Come to see the spectacular crowd!

The party begins at dusk, on October 31st.

I wasn't sure if I should show it to Trish. After the initial thrill of those first few Halloweens, we'd become disenchanted with Minnesota's approach to Halloween. Each year, we would try a different bar that advertised costume parties, but they were always disappointing. Most people did not wear costumes and came to get wasted. We agreed to give it up. Occasionally, we had our own private parties at home on Halloween, where I would dress up, but that didn't satisfy my need to be out expressing myself publicly. It felt very closeted and restricting to me. Besides, I was seriously into keeping the business on track, and I had plenty to occupy my mind. We had lots of success to be grateful for, and I did not want to upset that karma.

Now, looking at the Haunted Manors ad, I felt my old excitement returning.

"Hey, take a look at this." I slid the ad over to Trish.

"Halloween, really?" She looked at me like I was crazy. I knew she was thinking about all the effort we used to put into our costumes and how we always ended up sitting at our table while drunks bumped into each other on an overcrowded dance floor.

"Read it, Trish. It's not some random bar event, it's a big festival!"

She glanced down at the flyer, then back up. "We don't have time for costumes anyway, so what would it hurt to explore it once just to see if it's worth coming back next year?"

I stood up, grabbed the ad from her, and went up to the concierge desk and dropped the article on the counter in front of him.

"Do you know anything about this? Is it as great as advertised?"

Looking at me like the tourist I was, he reluctantly said, "Better."

"Really? Why is it better?" I asked.

"Go see for yourself! It's the most creative Halloween I've ever seen in South Florida, including South Beach, and that is saying a lot," he assured me.

"What and where is Wilton Manors?" I asked.

He suddenly became helpful, opening a map on his countertop.

"Wilton Manors is a predominantly gay township, and they sponsor the whole thing. They really go all out for Halloween. They take it very seriously," he said.

I was intrigued by the picture he'd painted of Wilton Manors. Surely, a gay community hosting a Halloween party would be one where most people participated and encouraged self-expression.

"This totally sounds like something we should check out," I said to Trish.

"Yes, it does sound like they know how to celebrate and have fun," she replied.

Arriving at twilight, we finally found a parking spot a few blocks off Wilton Drive. The drive was the main strip, which had been barricaded for the event. The lights came on in unison as if someone had pulled a huge circuit breaker to initiate the excitement. Stages lit up in preparation for performances, as did all the vendors' tents and booths up and down the streets. Music from all the clubs on Wilton Drive echoed in the streets. People were dancing onto the scene as the streets filled with partygoers. The atmosphere was festive, like Carnival in Rio. The main stage was set in a large parking lot that was once a K-Mart, which had cleverly been converted to a store called Gay-Mart. Wilton Manors embraced its residents.

As we approached, a very large group of city employees dressed as zombies took the stage and performed a well-choreographed rendition of the zombie dance from Michael Jackson's *Thriller* video. We were having fun already, and the night had just begun. A seemingly endless parade of costumed people showed off their creative costumes to each other and the wide-eyed onlookers who occupied the sidewalks.

These weren't the usual store-bought costumes. They were well-planned, elaborate, and often involved more than one person. One creature appeared to be a giant ogre of some kind.

Others under the costume exposed their seemingly severed heads under the person's arms. There were many over-the-top drag queens in extravagant make-up and huge wigs. Many came as group costumes, dressed as entire casts of characters from popular television shows and horror films.

"This is amazing," Trish shouted above the crowd noise.

"It is incredible, Honey, but very ironic," I shouted back.

"Why ironic?"

"Well, think about it, Trish. After all of the Halloween fails and finally giving up on it, we find the one place on earth I can totally let go and be uninhibited, and here we are, NOT in costume."

She thought about it for a second, grabbed my arm, and said, "But look what we've found here tonight. We can be prepared and come back next year in costume, now that we know."

I began planning our return trip the moment we got home. I put together a shimmering gold lame and beaded Cleopatra outfit with a shawl that was pleated, extending wings that I would unfold every few steps for drama. It was stunning.

The next year, stepping onto Wilton Drive in costume for the first time was everything I'd imagined and more. Every few feet, onlookers stopped me and asked to take my picture. I had a strong sense of freedom and confidence. I didn't have any fear of acceptance or the need to pretend this was just a costume. I was in my element.

"So many guys in drag," Trish noted as we walked through the crowd. "I wonder how many are here for the same reason we are?"

"Probably all of them," I said. "They are all just enjoying their freedom."

Back at our cottage around 11:00 pm, Trish was ready to call it a night. We had decided to stay on-site at a neighborhood resort that featured tastefully refurbished small homes as villas. We had quickly become good friends with the owner. In fact, earlier he'd invited us to an afterparty.

"You're having such a great time," Trish said. "Why don't you find our new friends and take them up on their invitation?"

That was so loving and understanding of her. She knew I wanted to get the most out of this, and she was right.

Walking down the Drive by myself, I stopped and chatted with others on the street and popped into a few clubs looking for my friends. I was in no hurry. I found such bliss in feeling like myself, and I cherished every moment along the way. I eventually found my friends and we had a few drinks in one of the clubs, then headed out for a 2 am breakfast down the street. It was so satisfying to be with new friends, enjoying their company and feeling like a complete woman the entire time.

We eventually walked back to the resort. Trish was fast asleep, and I was exhausted. I hadn't noticed how much my feet hurt until I stopped and took my heels off. I didn't bother to take my makeup or the rest of my costume off; I just collapsed into bed. Thus began our annual trip to Wilton Manors.

The next four years passed quickly. We left Minnesota completely. An opportunity to expand my business required a move to Chicago. It was very lucrative and worth the move. It would also prove to be life-altering. Planning our retirement, we bought a home on the Gulf Coast side of Florida in Fort Myers. We rented that out during the winter months for extra income. But each year, we still looked forward to our annual Halloween celebration in Wilton

Manors. Every year, I became bolder in my self-expression. It got to the point that I was bringing outfits for everyday street wear, should I abandon my fears and leave the house as the woman I wanted to be? No costumes, just me going about my day as I always felt I should.

On our third Wilton Manors Halloween, I had a life-changing experience. If Halloween fell on a Friday or Saturday, the partying began on Friday and lasted through Sunday. This one had been Saturday, and we had been here since Friday, staying at our usual resort. This extended weekend allowed a lot of opportunities to be a woman. I had costumes for all three nights, but also pushed the boundaries of going out as a woman during the daylight hours. I felt emboldened, compelled to see how it felt to be in everyday street clothes, not under the cover of being in costume.

Mornings, I'd put on a dress and makeup and walk six blocks to Starbucks to get coffee and our breakfast. I went to the grocery store and to the resort office to visit. We even went out for dinner each night before going out in costume. I used the excuse that I wanted to have my makeup on early so I wouldn't have to rush after dinner.

At the end of the weekend, I stood in front of the mirror, taking off my makeup and packing for home, reflecting on the last three days. The realization that I had lived the better part of this trip as a woman took me by the heart. I felt deeply saddened, knowing that I was leaving it behind. This wasn't like when I was a small child and didn't want to take my girl costume off after trick or treating; this was who I was. I didn't want to put the "Mike costume" back on.

When I was younger, I hoped that I would grow out of my desire to be a girl. I convinced myself that my feelings were false, and I was fooling myself or believing something that I did not fully understand. Surely, once I was married, established in business, had plenty of friends, and two homes, I would be happy. But packing up that day, I realized Halloween was just a temporary, disingenuous band-aid put on a much deeper wound. I never 'grew out of it' and I would never be satisfied hiding myself away any longer, no matter what I acquired or succeeded in.

The mirror reflected more than my image. The last three days revealed that this was not fading but intensifying. I was 61 years old and didn't need any further evidence that I had not been listening to my own heart. This long weekend lit the fuse, and it was burning fast, advancing quickly towards the powder keg.

Chapter Twelve:
Christmas Seasoning

---・---

We'd been back home in Chicago for a month since our last visit to Wilton Manors. The emotional effects of that trip lingered at the forefront of my mind, and I needed to put it out of my thoughts for a while.

The holiday season was kicking into high gear. This was a time when I could lighten up and be distracted from personal problems. Trish and I have loved our Christmases together since we met, and always fully celebrated the season. Christmastime was especially delightful in the city. This year, we spent three nights in a boutique hotel off North Michigan Avenue in the heart of Chicago's Gold Coast.

This tourist shopping district was always busy, but it was fun to move through the crowds during the holidays, checking out the window displays and stopping into the variety of stores. Our days went by fast. We enjoyed our favorite deep-dish pizza at Gino's, marveled over the night view from the Hancock Building observation deck, and were dazzled by a holiday musical at the Cadillac Palace Theater. Back home, we settled in for the rest of the season, visiting friends and attending church services.

When Christmas morning arrived, after our traditional breakfast, we headed to the family room and began exchanging gifts. Many of our gifts were things we'd asked each other for or understood that we needed as a couple, but each year we secretly bought one another an 'unexpected surprise,' something meaningful and personal.

I retrieved Trish's surprise from under the tree and placed it in her lap.

"Big box, what could this be?" she said.

Tearing the paper off, she saw the label and her eyes widened. She collapsed forward laughing.

"I'm glad it made you laugh, but that wasn't my intention," I joked.

"No, I love it, really. Thank you, but wait a second."

Trish got up and reached under the tree. She chose a box similar in size to the one I had given her, but wrapped in beautiful gold and silver foil, and then walked it over to me.

"Here's your unexpected gift, honey. Let's open together!"

I tore the wrapping paper off to reveal fancy graphics that looked familiar.

Estee Lauder's Complete Glamour Set!

"Oh My God, Trish! We got each other the same present."

"I thought you could have fun with this. Do you love it?" she said.

"Of course I do, that's why I bought one for you. It's a complete assortment of colors. The variety of makeup is amazing."

"This is too funny! I can't believe we got each other the exact same gift," Trish said.

"Especially this one. You win on the most unexpected, by a long shot," I declared.

We stood and hugged. I was deeply moved, but also puzzled. I didn't want Trish to see how much this meant to me, because I wasn't sure what that would mean for us. What did she mean by "I thought you could have fun with this"? Was this the green light for me to dress female more often? Was Trish signaling that she understood what I had been going through since our trip to Wilton Manors?

Our relationship was highly instinctive. We often knew quickly if the other person had something brewing inside, even if we hadn't discussed it. This was the first time Trish had gifted me anything feminine, and this was *so* feminine:

an elaborate selection of makeup. We placed our open gifts back under the tree, cleaned up the wrapping paper, and prepared for the rest of Christmas day.

I felt like a child who just received the best present possible, then had to put it away without playing with it... while aching to try it out. I was afraid to delve deeper into the meaning of the gift; I convinced myself that she gave it to me for next year's Halloween. I looked forward to the time when I could try out all the variety of my new makeup. I wouldn't have to wait much longer for my first opportunity to check it out, but I would be doing it secretly.

Shortly after the New Year, Trish left for Florida while I stayed home to take care of business and our dog, Jake. I would be able to do most of my business from home. I had established customers whom I could work with from anywhere that had a computer and internet service. Trish would get our condominium ready for the seasonal renters we had coming in February. She could spend time with her Florida friends and enjoy the sunshine. She would be gone all month, giving me lots of time to reflect on what I'd been through emotionally in the last several weeks.

The first morning, I woke up early — long before any of my customers would be in their offices.

I was going through my closet, and there was the Estée Lauder makeup that Trish gave me for Christmas. What harm would it be if I tried it out? She'd bought it for me to use. I brought it into the bathroom and opened it. The vibrant palettes of color, gleaming and pristine, invited me to try them. I never had such a beautiful selection at my fingertips.

I retrieved a storage bin from the closet that contained my collection of previous Halloween costumes and found wigs and clothes. I shook out an auburn-colored short-bob style wig, placed it on my head, and brushed it out. I found a leather skirt I'd bought for one of the costumes and slid into it. I couldn't find a top, so I slipped on a sexy, black satin bra, and the outfit was complete for now.

Seeing myself in the mirror, I glowed. My senses were heightened. I felt feminine, pretty, and peaceful all at once. My thoughts were clear and quiet. I was at ease with myself and didn't question right, wrong, or why. It was as though I was right where I should be, what I should be.

I went downstairs to the kitchen and enjoyed my morning coffee, feeling complete and content.

Throwing on a sweater, I stayed in this outfit as the day progressed. I realized that I needed more than "costume" clothes. Even though Trish responded positively to my desire to wear dresses, wigs, and even makeup, I was accustomed to exploring the woman within me only when alone. I wanted to take the next few days to live out my dreams.

I surrendered control to an online shopping spree. In those moments, I saw myself as a real woman who bought everything she'd been deprived of. I was as jubilant as Julia Roberts in *Pretty Woman*, joyfully going store-to-store purchasing all the beautiful clothes and accessories that she could never have. I purchased skirts, blouses, dresses, wigs, and a variety of accessories to complete each outfit. They were all shipped overnight, making them available at once.

Going about my daily business with my customers, suppliers, and shipping companies for the next few days was a breeze. I never enjoyed my work more. As a woman, I was relaxed, focused, and entirely on my game. It got dark early that time of year, and I braved taking Jake for his nightly walk, still dressed female. It was cold, and I was bundled up, but it was a bold step to take in my own neighborhood. I didn't share any of this with Trish in our nightly phone conversation. *Let her enjoy herself and not worry about me,* I thought.

In my nightgown, lying awake, I was conflicted. Was I deceiving Trish by not sharing this? Then there was the inner turmoil that had followed me throughout my life. On one hand, there was this woman within who felt alive and natural when given the chance to express herself. On the other hand, there was this guy who fought like hell to suppress her.

This "other self" that I had constructed and fortified to present a male image was resisting. I asked myself, "What is wrong with you? and What are you planning to do with all these clothes when Trish is back? Have you completely lost your mind?" Would I ever reach a point where I would reconcile the two and be a whole person? Remarkable coincidences would take place in the next few days that would provide a gateway to answers for many of my questions.

Chapter Thirteen:
A New Year, A New Opportunity

The next day, having completed my morning routine of getting dressed, sipping coffee, and reading my emails, I was busy working in my home office. I never watched morning TV talk shows, but one was playing in the background. The reporter grabbed my attention when she announced, "Coming next: the shocking news about Bruce Jenner's drastic life changes."

Bruce was a gold-medal-winning Olympic triathlete and someone I admired, so I waited for the story. After the commercial, the network morning host returned and declared, "Bruce Jenner disclosed that he has been transitioning from male to female and will no longer be known as Bruce, but rather as 'Caitlyn Jenner.'"

What? Had I heard that right? I was awestruck!

The anchor continued with details of Caitlyn's story, showing a split screen of Bruce/Caitlyn. There was the famous photo of Bruce with his arms raised high in the air as he crossed the finish line of the medal-winning race, next to a photo shoot of Caitlyn in the now-famous pose in a white satin corset. I could not believe what I was hearing and seeing. I froze in front of the TV as the story unfolded. The reporter continued with details about Caitlyn's struggle growing up at a time when you had to hide your feelings, and there was no definition of what it meant to be transgender.

The story was too familiar. Growing up as Bruce, she repressed her feelings through sports and competition. She had the need to prove her maleness and went all-out at every opportunity. She wanted a life like everyone else and knew that wasn't possible if anyone found out how she really felt inside. Our stories were exactly the same, if you leave aside her wealth and Olympic medals! I was impressed by her courage and the risk she had taken coming out.

I was 62 years of age, watching this, knowing Caitlyn was a few years older than me. That was pivotal because it pointed out that I was *not* too old to make changes in my life. It was also a living example that time does not change what is in your heart and imprinted in your brain cells from birth. You are who you are, your *entire* life.

With all that success, fame, and athletic prowess, she still had to face the inescapable truth. What chance did I have of going on without facing my own? Just then, a customer emailed, and I couldn't dwell on it anymore.

Later that day, I retrieved the mail from our front door mailbox. I saw an important notice from my health insurance provider and opened it immediately. They were informing me that the coverage in my policy for the new year would cover additional psychiatric care for conditions not previously covered. Among those new areas of coverage highlighted was treatment for gender dysphoria.

I sat down in the living room, reliving the events since Wilton Manors. There had been times within those days that I prayed for answers and needed guidance. More than once, I'd prayed for a sign.

Now, those signs were flashing like neon lights in Times Square.

This confluence of significant circumstances involving gender issues led me to believe that the time to act had arrived. I'd been running from myself my entire life. Now was the time to step forward and be completely honest with myself. If this were not the time, it would never come.

I couldn't do this without professional help. I needed an expert who specialized in gender therapy. I googled gender therapists near me and was surprised to see so many in the Chicago area. I would have to choose carefully. I needed someone who understood gender dysphoria but could also understand the multiple issues I had developed by hiding it for so many years.

I read several reviews and chose the one that had the experience I was looking for. I was also comforted by the name—Compassionate Counseling. I made the call the next day.

Chapter Fourteen:
The Doctor Will See You Now

———— • ————

Still twelve minutes to wait. My car was idling, heater on, parked in front of Compassionate Counseling. I'd only been there a short time, but it seemed like hours. What was I doing here anyway? I hadn't discussed any of this with Trish, and here I was, anxiously awaiting my first therapy session. My conscience was telling me to drive away, talk to Trish about it, and come back another time.

But I was there for a reason. I needed help immediately and couldn't put it off another day. I'll get a preliminary introduction to therapy and get to know the therapist first. If it felt right, I'd bring Trish up to speed when she got home. Or so I told myself.

My apprehension wasn't eased by the fact that I was parked in front of a house in a residential neighborhood. My vision of an institutional-looking medical office building with a discreet entrance to a psychiatric inner sanctum was quickly dashed as I gazed up and down the typically suburban streets of Bolingbrook, Illinois.

"Be thoughtful of other patients' privacy. Do not be more than ten minutes early. Enter through the side door and wait in the outer office." The doctor's instructions had made that clear.

Ten minutes before three. I turned off the car and stepped into the blustery January air. The frigid wind rushed down my throat and took my breath away as I hurried around to the side entrance. Just as I opened the outer storm door, a violent gust of wind took hold of it, almost pulling it off the hinges. My heart raced as I wrestled it back, opened the inner door, and stepped inside. I closed both and took a deep, steadying breath.

Inside, the waiting area was small. A few chairs, lamps, and a long table with various brochures fanned across the length and width. They were provided by transgender support groups, medical doctors, electrolysis professionals, and other organizations in the gender community services network.

I wouldn't allow myself to go through them. I was like a small child at a wake who couldn't get close to the dead body; it might be contagious. I feared that if I read them, I would be assuming a conclusion before I began my therapy.

I unzipped my coat and sat, awaiting my turn. I heard shuffling and voices inside. The patient before me was finished and walking down the interior hallway towards the front door. So that's how she keeps privacy, I thought. In through the side, out the front.

A moment later, the door to the waiting area opened.

"You must be Michael. I'm Doctor Wilke, but my patients call me Dr. Deb. Come in and have a seat." She pointed at two chairs opposite one another.

"Yes, I am. Nice to meet you. Over there?" I said, pointing at the two high-backed leather chairs.

"Yes, and please make yourself comfortable."

That seemed impossible right then, but I took another deep breath. After we'd both seated ourselves, she looked down at her notes.

"I see by the profile you sent that you've been struggling with gender issues for a long time."

"As long as I can remember. First memories are from when I was about four to five years old."

"And how old are you now, if you don't mind my asking?" she asked, continuing to take notes.

"I'll be sixty-three in a few months. Is it unusual to see somebody of my age coming in for their first session?" I asked.

She paused. "Nothing unusual, Michael. There's no guideline for when someone chooses to seek help. We are all different people traveling down different paths. There are personal circumstances that prevent us from getting help, and a variety of reasons for the why and when. None of them need justification."

I was impressed with her answer and began to relax.

"But you probably don't have 62-year-olds lined up outside your door, do you?" I said.

"No, I don't," she laughed. "But I will say it will be interesting and refreshing to work with someone close to my own age. Most of my patients are very young and don't have the experiences we have. They are not always clear on what they need."

"That's what we all have in common, regardless of age, right?" I joked.

"Yes, I know," she said. "It's just going to be interesting to hear your story. A lifetime of experiences dealing with gender dysphoria while trying to survive in a world that had little understanding and no tolerance of the subject," she replied.

"And I'm happy to finally talk to someone with your experience and expertise, so it should be productive," I replied.

"Let me ask you this, Michael," she said, sitting back in her chair. "What are your goals here? What do you hope to accomplish?"

I thought for a moment. I wasn't prepared for that question right off the bat.

"I need to define some things before I can figure out where I'm going from here. I know how I've felt for so many years, but I don't understand the reason. I'm confused by all of the variations in males who dress female. Seems like the lines are blurred between transgenders, transvestites, drag queens, or others who might just dress for thrills."

"There's a lot to talk about on that, and we will as we get into it," she replied.

"Great, because I need you to tell me exactly what it is that I am."

I watched her expression darken.

"I will *never* do that!" She was silent for a long moment, then her voice softened.

"How about this, Michael, let's give this the time and attention it takes together. We will explore the last sixty-two years of your life, making no assumptions. Eventually, we will reach a point when you have the answers for yourself. Only you can determine who or what you are, *but* I can help you unravel the mystery that will make it clear to you. Does that sound fair?"

I was surprised and impressed with the conviction she displayed. She had gained my trust.

"Yes, it does. How will we know when we're done?" I said.

Smiling easily, she said, "When there's nothing left to say."

"That's straightforward enough for me," I said.

Throughout the rest of the session, she asked me about my history and why I thought I was stifling my true self.

"Given the time you grew up in and the stigma of feeling different, I can understand why you've held everything inside for so long, but can you elaborate on why you think you did?" she asked.

"So many reasons. I couldn't envision what kind of life it would have been if everyone knew how I felt. I had negative feedback from dressing up when I was a small child, so I held everything deep inside. No one in my world knew anything about being transgender or what it meant, not even me."

"Yes, those were the dark ages of gender and sexuality," she said. "How about family, do you have siblings?"

"Yes, I do, Doctor Deb. I have four brothers and three sisters. I'm the youngest of eight. The next three older than me are all guys, then two sisters, one more brother, and the eldest child, a sister. It's such a range of ages, like a two-tier family. I grew up with the three brothers closest to my age. We did everything together as kids. I loved all of my brothers and sisters and was terrified they would find me out and disown me, even though I knew they loved me as much as I loved them. How could I expect them to understand something about me that I couldn't understand?"

"That's not an unreasonable fear, especially for a child," she said. "What about your parents?"

"I loved and admired my mom and dad. I had so much respect for them and how hard they worked, how they lived their beliefs, and made sure we had what we needed to succeed in life. All of us are successful because of them."

"How about now? Are they still alive?"

"No, they were killed by a drunk driver when I was a teenager. Being the youngest, I was the only one still living at home at the time."

"That is horrible!" she said, "So much to deal with as a teenager."

"Well, my whole family was equally devastated. It was tragic for us all and drew us even closer together. I became more resolute in burying my gender issues. It all seemed so small and inconsequential after that, but I didn't realize at the time that it would never go away."

"No, it certainly does not. We are who we are forever." She looked down at her notes, flipping through the pages. "I see you're married. What does your wife think about you being here?"

"Trish is at our place in Florida all month. She doesn't know I'm doing this. I felt the need for help now and thought I would get started, then tell her about it later."

"Interesting, but not unusual. It is a monumental leap to take, and sometimes more difficult to talk with those closest to us before we understand what's going on. You will tell her soon, though, right?" she said.

"Yes, I'll wait until I've got a handle on where we're going first," I replied.

"Your choice, you'll know when it feels right," she said, then stood by the door. "Our time is up for today. I suggest we meet as often as possible; there's lots to cover here. Can you come two or three times a week?"

"Sure. I'm eager to learn as much as I can. I'm not getting younger."

As I stood up and stepped closer to Doctor Deb to shake hands and say goodbye, a wave of emotion washed over me. I started to cry unexpectedly.

"I'm sorry, Doctor Deb. The reality struck me that I'm sixty-two years old, and this is the first time in my life I've been able to talk to someone openly about what I've had locked inside of me forever. This is a watershed moment if there ever was one. I've been running from myself all my life, and I need to stop now."

She moved in quickly and gave me a hug. I could see her eyes watering.

"That's why you're here, you *have* stopped running. And you are no longer hiding from anything. It took courage to come here, and we're going to do this together."

"Thanks, Doctor. I'll set my next appointment soon."

Chapter Fifteen: Definition

I had a few days to absorb the first session with Dr. Deb. I trusted her completely, but still felt vulnerable. Whatever we discovered together would change my life. Did I really want the truth? In my heart, I did, but my practical mind was resisting. Would I ever allow myself to accept what might be revealed? I had to remain calm and keep an open mind.

"Let's pick up where we left off," Dr. Deb said at our next session.

I settled into my chair, taking a sip from the Starbucks I brought along. It was a pacifier for me, calming my nerves.

"Sure. I think we were talking about defining myself," I replied.

"Yes, it's a difficult thing to do—especially after concealing your feelings for so many years. The longer you keep them under wraps, the longer it takes to unravel," she explained.

"I'm confused about how one determines if they are actually transgender, as opposed to being a crossdresser. I have times when I'm certain that I am a woman, and others when I deny myself. I won't accept it, and I convince myself that it's something I do compulsively," I said.

She paused, and I could see by the look on her face that I had struck an important subject.

"That's a great place to start. In our first session, you asked me to tell you what it is you are, and now I know what's confusing you. I understand the source of your frustration. You want me to define the distinction between cross-dressing for pleasure and actual gender dysphoria. Keep in mind, I'm speaking generally when trying to define the difference. There are various reasons why people cross-dress," she said.

This was what I needed to hear. "That would be a helpful start," I replied.

"The best way to describe it is this: Many cross-dressers do so for the pleasure of the moment. It may be sexual pleasure, or just a feeling of well-being and escape. They typically start doing this after puberty. They are comfortable in the bodies they were born in and have no desire to make changes to their physical gender. Now, that does not mean that some are not transgender; that's where it becomes confusing," she said.

I listened, still wondering where I was on the spectrum.

"So, in your experience, how have YOU determined the difference?" I asked.

She put one finger up in the air, as if a light had just turned on in her head.

"I was hoping you would ask; this is important. Most people with gender dysphoria are not comfortable with their given physical gender from early on in life and need to permanently change their gender. That is a major difference. We will get into your past as we move forward, but this is a true point of distinction," she replied.

I was relieved to hear that. I knew how I'd felt my entire life, but was still confused about something else.

"What about the sexual arousal component? If I became aroused when dressed up, does that mean I'm not transgender?" I asked.

I felt so naive. Was this a stupid question? I hoped to have known myself better at this stage of life.

"No, it does not. This is where the danger lies. You cannot assume anything yet. Sexuality is part of being human, and it manifests itself in different situations. My belief is simple. If you keep something hidden and have this huge secret, it is stimulating when you allow it to become a form of expression. Everyone has sexual desires. Why they are stimulated is not always clear," she said.

I recalled the many times Trish and I returned from our night out on Halloween and experienced the most incredible sex, multiple times. At those times, I wasn't sure why I was so hyper-stimulated and didn't care. Afterwards, I would wonder if I was dressing just for that stimulation, but then again, my feelings of gender dysphoria had begun long before I reached puberty.

Dr. Deb had a wry smile on her face, which told me I was feeding her the information she needed.

"I know it's confusing for every one of my transgender patients. Many have shared the same concerns with me, but don't let your sexual feelings lead you to believe you are not transgender. We won't conclude anything just yet, but what you've told me so far is very helpful. If you felt this way that early in life, you are likely suffering from gender dysphoria. You don't display the traits of a cross-dressing male," she said.

I was happy to hear that. I felt validated and knew we were on the right track and making progress. The topic of crossdressing reminded me of when I'd reached out to the University of Minnesota for gender help years ago, and they referred me to the president of a Minneapolis crossdressers club. I explained it all to Dr. Deb.

"What offended you?" she said, after I'd told her my experience and reaction.

"Well, I was reaching out for help for the first time, and they shuttled me off to a group I had absolutely no interest in being a part of. I was interested in talking with someone who understands gender dysphoria, like I am doing here with you. Instead, they somehow thought being in a room full of guys dressed as women would answer my questions."

"I'm surprised they did that; the University of Minnesota has always been at the forefront of Gender Studies." She put one hand out in front of her, pausing me so she could take notes. She was writing feverishly, as though I'd said something significant on the topic.

"Anything else you can remember about why you felt so disappointed?" she said.

Stretching my back to relieve tension from sitting, I put my elbows on my thighs and leaned forward.

"Yes. I don't have anything personal against a club like that, and I'm not judging. They can do what they want in private, but it's just not for me. Going to a monthly 'dress-up' party with a bunch of guys would just be stepping into a bigger, more populated closet. What then? You return to the same old frustrations you've been dealing with until next month's get-together? When I woke up the day after, I'd still be male with the same problems, right?"

Still taking notes, she said, "Let's back up just a few minutes. We were talking about the difference between crossdressers and those who are transgendered. This is a defining moment, so I'll clarify what I said. Most crossdressers don't begin doing so until puberty. Sometimes it's only for sexual excitement, sometimes it's just for fun, but it is not done because they identify as female and *need* to express those feelings outwardly and permanently. Do you see where I'm headed with this?"

"Yes, we have talked about how I knew how I felt since I was four or five years old, and just now how I felt about how upset I was that I wasn't going to be helped by occasionally crossdressing. I didn't like the idea of just dipping my toes in the water; I wanted to dive into the ocean."

"What a perfect metaphor, Michael. That brings up another question for you. Again, the first time we were here, you said you wanted me to *tell* you exactly what it is you are. Why do you need me to tell you something you already know?"

I could tell by the tone of her voice that she knew the answer and was making a point she wanted me to confirm in my own words. I gathered my thoughts, then spoke words that cleared the path for her to help me.

"In my heart of hearts, I know I am a woman. The problem is—and always has been—that I'm of two minds. One is logical and practical; the other, emotional and sensitive. The logical side has dominated my life, served me well in business, and helped me carry on masquerading as a man. But it's not the truth; it's not who I am. I have been in this endless cycle of acceptance and denial—acceptance and denial—as long as I've been alive. I create doubt, convincing myself that dressing as a woman is just for fun or a passing whim, but I know better. So when I told you, 'I want you to tell me exactly what it is I am,' I was really saying, help me. I need an explanation or confirmation of my feelings to break this cycle of self-doubt."

"Excellent!" she exclaimed. "That is the starting point we established here today. That is the self-awareness we're going to build on."

The weight of the world lifted off my shoulders. I'd finally spoken the words. I'd freely admitted to another human being that I really understood myself to be a woman.

"When you say 'build on,' Dr.Deb, where do we begin doing that?" I asked.

"*Reconstruct* is a better word. I have some homework for you." She raised her hands, drawing a huge rectangle in the air in front of her. "Have you ever seen those large collages of photos people put together for someone's graduation, or some other momentous occasion?"

"Sure, lots of times," I said. I wondered what this had to do with me.

"Ok, I want you to compile images that meant something to you when you were a child. They can be a collection of family photos, magazine clippings, photos from books, or even old movie posters. Anything that left an impression, or you thought was cool... and attach them to a board of your own."

"Why?" I asked.

"Together we're going to understand who you are."

That would be a first for me, I thought.

Chapter Sixteen: Picture This

After the last session, I didn't waste any time. I stopped at a large used-book and vintage magazine shop on my way home. I found magazines from the '50s and '60s with great advertising pictures, copies of *Look* magazine that featured many iconic photos, and a coffee table book that was a history of Hollywood in pictures. That book was ideal for my project. It highlighted the best films of major movie stars, including pictures and posters.

After hours of snipping, I sat back, amazed at the range of subjects. I'd clipped out everything from Barbie dolls and Cinderella to James Bond and the Beatles. Every movie featuring men masquerading as women was represented, including *Some Like It Hot, Myra Breckenridge, Switch*, and *Where's Charlie*. I clipped all my favorite glamor queens I'd admired from those old movies. I loved the hair, makeup, and wonderful fashions, especially the magnificent gowns. I'd imagined myself being that beautiful.

I found many black-and-white family photos. Most of them reminded me of the fun times we had and how close I had been to my brothers and sisters. I remembered all the sports we played and the fact that we competed hard against one another. The sense of humor we shared, as well as the strong bond. We stuck up for each other in every situation.

Fastening everything I'd cut out to a large piece of cardboard I'd fashioned from a shipping box, I realized that despite feelings of gender dysphoria, I had been an incredibly lucky kid. I had parents who loved and cared about the kind of person I would be, siblings whom I loved and shared good and troubled times with, and I had been equipped with everything I needed to become a successful human being if I made the effort. Too many kids didn't have that. I was beginning to see the genius of Dr. Deb's project, and I couldn't wait to discuss it.

In the days between sessions, I talked with Trish several times a day, as usual. I didn't break my silence on the therapy, knowing it needed to be discussed in person when she returned home. There was part of me that wanted to tell her I was really getting help... but then on the other hand, I felt guilty for doing this while she was away, keeping her in the dark.

Stepping into Dr. Deb's office the next week, I braced the large cardboard collage of pictures on the chair next to mine, where she could view it entirely.

"Done so soon?" she said.

"Yeah, I really got into it and was able to find lots of good material."

She moved closer and leaned in to get a better look. "Interesting assortment of images. Are the black-and-whites your family?"

"Yes, Dr. Deb, I am showing my age. All my early photos are pre-color film."

"I can relate," she said, looking through them carefully.

Picking up the board and setting it aside, she returned to her chair. "What did you learn doing this project, Michael?"

"That you are very clever, Doctor."

"Really," she laughed, "how so?"

"The therapy was doing the project. Compiling information, thinking about which photos and ads were relevant and why. It wasn't just looking at old photos and pop culture iconic movies. It was looking into them more deeply. Why was this one more relevant than another? What did this *really* mean to me at the time? Sure, I'd remembered many of these things at various times over the years, but never really looked at them collectively. It painted the bigger picture for me."

"Wonderful. And what stood out, what did you eventually conclude?"

"Two things. One, I desperately wanted to be a girl. Two, I was not an unhappy child. Even with all those things on my mind, I lived a wonderful life, up to a certain point."

"That is great awareness! Can you tell me to what point, and why things changed for you?" she asked.

"About the time I hit fifteen, sixteen. My happiness was gone. My body changed, and my mind was not in tune with it. I began to realize the full effects of gender dysphoria. I didn't know what to call it or what it meant at the time, but I was anxious and disgusted with myself. I despised becoming more masculine. I could no longer fool myself into believing there was any chance of being a girl. I shot up to over six feet tall in high school and felt awkward and uncomfortable in my own skin. It was hopeless."

"That must have been awful," she said. "But you survived. When did things change? Was there anything you remember that got you through those times?"

"Things kept getting worse. I became depressed, didn't care about myself, and got into serious trouble with the law when I was 18," I replied.

I went on to explain the tragic loss of my parents, the resulting guilt I felt about my gender struggles, and the tailspin my life went into. I felt flushed and was sweating as I recalled the worst days of my life. I stood up for a moment, walking around the room, acting like I was just stretching my legs.

"Sorry, I needed to move. My back and legs are killing me today," I said.

She waited patiently for me to return to my chair. She understood the anxiety of the moment and gracefully allowed it to pass without showing concern.

"I think I'm beginning to understand how you justified your self-denial. It's easy to see why you didn't allow yourself to believe you were something you couldn't grasp. You were in shock and had all the emotional baggage you could carry."

"That's a fair description," I said. "I was also questioning my faith. I couldn't understand why this happened. I was angry, and it took time for me to reconcile myself to God."

"That is a good place to start next time, Michael. I think we've made great strides already."

We had made progress. Not only did the picture board reveal how I viewed myself as a child, but it also allowed Dr. Deb to take it a few years beyond. She had a vivid background on where and why things changed dramatically in my life. Now that she understood exactly where I came from, maybe she could help get me where I needed to go.

Chapter Seventeen:
Images Equal Perception

Three more sessions with Dr. Deb had gone by. I was sitting at home dissecting everything we had discussed since our first meeting. There was much to absorb, and therapy was far from complete, but I was certain the sessions were helping me tremendously. I knew where I stood now, and why it had taken me so long to get here.

Many of my questions were answered, and many of my fears and concerns were eliminated. Trish would be home soon, and I was trying to organize my thoughts. How would I explain all of this to her? I leaned onto the back cushion of the sofa and placed my foot on the coffee table, bracing the posterboard collage of pictures so I could analyze it.

The more I looked at the movie and television clippings that depicted men posing as women, the more it hit me how desperate I'd been to find anyone who was anything like me. I could now see that these were not the best examples . . . they were the *only* ones.

I began to think about the media's influence on how I dealt with my struggle to understand myself. Equally important, how did it influence the perception society had of anyone who expressed gender variation? The clippings I'd chosen were from movies and TV shows I'd seen when I was young. In one photo, Tom Hanks clutched a leather handbag and pursed his lips into the camera. It was from the show *Bosom Buddies,* in which two male roommates lost their lease and couldn't afford to live anywhere in NYC, except in a building that was restricted to females. Posing as women, they were accepted into the apartment and became the subjects of every stereotype and embarrassing situation the writers could imagine. They were men dressed as women, and therefore, they deserved to be humiliated for a few cheap laughs.

When I'd been with a group of people watching TV and this show came on, I sank into my chair and cringed. My anxiety level rose to the point where I would excuse myself and sit in the bathroom for several minutes to regain my composure. I couldn't allow anyone to see my embarrassment.

Yet despite this, when Dr. Deb asked me to show her images that inspired me, I'd included Tom Hanks alongside stills from *Some Like It Hot.* Why had I made that choice? On the couch, I thought about how, after *Bosom Buddies,* movie characterizations evolved into darker, psycho-killer depictions of trans people in the films *Dressed to Kill* and *The Silence of the Lambs*.

The villain in the former attacked and slashed his female victims to death with a butcher knife. This murderous soul only hurt others while dressed as a woman. This implied a psychopathic link between thrill killing and cross-dressing.

The latter's psycho-killer kidnapped, tormented, and skinned his female victims, wearing their skins to make himself appear female. While *The Silence of the Lambs* denies that the villain, Buffalo Bill, is transgender, it is not possible for the viewer to separate the imagery, mannerisms, or desire of Bill to wear his victim's skin to become a woman from the idea of being trans. When those films came out, they disgusted me. Even then, before I had words to describe my own identity, I knew this wasn't who I was or what trans people were. These are fictional characters, but such depictions were so damaging to a misunderstood minority, who comprise an incredibly tiny percentage of the population.

Most people have never met a trans person and had nothing else to go on but this trans-cinematic legacy of exploitation. Such depictions underscored Hollywood's appetite for profit, which trumped all sensitivity towards the transgender condition. But things were changing. Shifting on the couch, I set aside the poster board.

Revisiting the negative impressions allowed me to see how much things had changed. The media was putting forth positive stories in the news and creating stronger fictional characters in the movies. Caitlyn Jenner's story was handled with kindness and sensitivity as it broke into a sensational sports and news story. The trans character in *Orange Is the New Black,* played by Laverne Cox, was closer to reality than anything I had seen before.

Enlightened by therapy, clarity in my own thoughts and feelings, and the reaffirming images coming from the media, I could now see a path towards change. I had come to terms with myself and was unlocking the door to my personal prison. In legal terms, I had made the case to myself, and the verdict was in. I was a transwoman, and it was time to come out.

How would I tell the woman I had loved since the day I met her over thirty years ago? Trish knew about my passion for "dressing up," but as far as I knew, she had never imagined I was actually trans. Still, she'd been with me when we decided to seek help through the University of Minnesota. There was some precedent. I'd included her in the early steps in my journey, I reassured myself, hoping somehow that would lessen the betrayal. I'd vowed to be her husband forever, and I would be asking her to accept me as her female spouse.

This was going to be the most difficult thing I'd ever done. I couldn't stand the possibility of losing her. It would shock and hurt her, and I couldn't bear the idea of doing that. Still, I'd gone too far to turn back. I couldn't undo what I had done or ignore what I learned about myself. If I told her, it could destroy us. If I didn't tell her, I would be hiding something that I was now certain of, and that could destroy us. I was in a "damned if I do/damned if I don't" spot. I made up my mind. Trish would be home soon.

Chapter Eighteen: Trish, Coming Home

"I can't tell you that there is no straightforward way to break this to Trish; I can't tell you what kind of reaction to expect. I can only caution you that less than fifty percent of couples survive a revelation of this kind, and I have dealt with over three hundred transitions."

Dr. Deb's warning was repeating in my mind as nervous energy fueled the cleaning of our three-level townhome. I had been up and downstairs, doing laundry, dusting shelves, and preparing for Trish to return from Florida. It was a running joke between us that we cleaned house when we were upset. I would often say that she pissed me off on purpose, just to get the house in order. I smiled just a little, thinking the sparkling clean floor would alert her that something was going on. I always left the floors up to her. The message alert sounded from my cell. I ran over to my phone to check it out.

"Hi honey, I'm here, waiting at baggage claim. I texted the limo service, and they're on the way!"

"Great, can't wait to see you. Let me know when you're on the road, so I know your driver arrived."

The clock was officially ticking. I would be happy to see her again, but I dreaded what I was going to tell her. More of Dr. Deb's advice came to mind. "Allow Trish time to settle in and relax for a few days before dropping this in her lap. Let her adjust to being back home awhile."

Great advice, but she'd only known me for a short time. What she didn't know about me was that if I had something to say, I couldn't hold back. If I had a surprise for Trish, I would give it to her before its intended time. She would tease that I would give away the nuclear codes if they were a surprise gift.

But this was a profoundly serious surprise, one that could change our lives and destroy our relationship.

I had considered putting aside what I had discovered and going on as if I had all my life to spare Trish the painful truth. Would I risk our marriage by being honest, counting on the strength of our love to get us through?

In our thirty years together, I had always put her feelings above my own, and now I had taken on something monumental without giving her the benefit of discussion or warning. In this instance, however, I had felt that there was no time for second-guessing what I had learned about my despair in therapy. I had been driven to find answers and could not be selective in their truths. I had reached a tipping point and had confronted myself for a very legitimate reason. I sought out Dr. Deb's expertise because I needed answers. Now that I had a preliminary understanding, it would be impossible to deny help and the hope of resolution. I concluded that keeping this from her would only make things worse.

Gazing out the front window, I could see the black stretch limo pull in front of our house. I hurried down to help with the luggage and welcome her home. We embraced and kissed while the limo driver started into the house with her bags. Jake, our golden retriever, was so excited to see her, he slipped out the door and headed right for Trish, nearly knocking her over.

"Well, I'm happy to see you, too, Jake!" Trish laughed.

"He's been waiting for you right along with me. Let's get everything in the house. Did you eat on the plane?"

"Just a snack," she replied.

"Let's go grab a bite then."

All through dinner, I couldn't stop thinking about what I had to say and when I should say it. I felt the need to tell her building in my gut like hot lava boiling inside a volcano. It was only a matter of time before I erupted. Back at home now, we sat across from each other on opposing living room love seats.

"So, what all did you do while I was gone?" Trish asked.

"Well," I replied in a tone that indicated I'd done something she wouldn't like.

Uncrossing her legs and leaning towards me, she tensed up. "Well, what? Is something wrong?"

"No. I just have something to tell you that's hard to talk about. And I'm not sure where to begin or how to say it."

Now she looked frightened and confused, obviously sensing the serious nature of the impending conversation.

"What is it? Are you in trouble?" she asked.

"No. Something's been troubling me, though, and I couldn't hold it back any longer without seeking help."

"What kind of help are you talking about? What's going on here?" Her voice was breaking now.

"Right after you left for Florida, I received a letter from Blue Cross. It said they were now covering psychological therapy. I did some research online and found a local doctor who specializes in gender identity therapy, and I started seeing her a few weeks ago. I've had several sessions already."

The color left her face, and she looked as if I had just punched her in the stomach. She seemed devastated, and I hadn't gotten to the worst of it yet.

"Who is this doctor? Why did you need to do this? What are you two talking about? I have so many questions, I don't know where to begin."

"Her name is Dr. Deborah Wilke. She's a therapist who has many years of experience in gender identity counseling. She is highly recommended and has great credentials."

I felt selfish and ashamed explaining this to her. I could see I had hurt her with this news and hated myself for doing it.

I got up and sat next to her, clutching her hands in mine.

"It was hard for me to make this choice, but I knew I had to act on it. I know it's not the way we've done things all our lives together. I couldn't tell you about it until I had a better understanding of what was going on."

"And do you?" she said abruptly. "Have a better understanding so you can tell me just what *is* going on?" she asked.

Admitting to her what I could not accept within myself for so long was difficult. My throat tightened as I choked back tears so I wouldn't further alarm her.

"It's too soon for any conclusions, but all indicators strongly point toward my being transgender."

She released my hand and shot up off the sofa.

"Transgender? How did this go from a letter from our insurance company to you being transgender?"

She was pacing the room now, looking at me for an answer.

"It wasn't just the letter. That just gave me a pathway to get help. It was a series of events going back to last Halloween in Florida and, more recently, seeing people in the news like Caitlyn Jenner and Laverne Cox being accepted publicly. These are huge changes in attitudes socially, and I found myself being jealous, asking, Why not me? When would my time come?"

She paused for a second to take a breath and absorb everything.

"I just don't understand. I mean, I knew that you loved dressing up every Halloween and at home sometimes. I thought it was just fun, and never once did I consider that it was anything more than that. I know we looked into it a few years ago when the University referred you to someone, but I thought we were far beyond exploring anything more."

"There is more to it, and I don't understand everything about myself or how to deal with that. I've been wrestling with this for too many years, and I can't handle not knowing any longer."

She leaned on the fireplace mantle and looked down, shaking her head.

"And what does that mean to us, to our life together? Are you talking about becoming a woman, or are you leaving me?"

Now I could see tears coming down her cheek as the worst-case scenario played out in her head.

"No, honey. I don't know where this is going or what it is that I am, but I promise you that I will *not* do anything or act on anything that is going to destroy us. If you want me to stop therapy, I will do that right now."

Visibly upset, she stepped in front of me and walked over to the staircase heading to the upstairs bedroom.

"All of this is too much to deal with right now. I'm going upstairs to read before bed."

Frustrated that this ended without more discussion, I raised my voice. "Wait a minute, I don't think we've completely talked about this."

Halfway up the stairs, she glanced back at me with pain and bewilderment in her eyes. I got the message loud and clear that I should stay downstairs, and we'd talked all we were going to for now.

Later, I crept into the bedroom and quietly crawled into bed with her, knowing she had fallen asleep. Tired from travel and shaken by what I told her, she needed sleep, and I stayed on the far side of the bed so I wouldn't wake her.

It's not unusual for me to be up and working at 5:30 every day. I do much of my business with overseas companies, and the time difference works out for me in the early hours.

The next morning, however, I was working at my computer at 4:00 am. I had had a restless night, thinking about what the next morning would be like.

By 8:00, I began to wonder if Trish was awake and purposely staying upstairs to avoid me or just sleeping in.

I went into the kitchen, threw some bread in the toaster, and then heard Trish coming down the stairs.

"Good morning, you want toast or something?" I asked.

"No, I'm not hungry."

"All right, let me know if you want anything."

As I spread the toast with butter, I could see Trish in the living room, staring at me as if I were a stranger to her. I felt like she was reassessing me and our marriage. Mornings had always been an easy, fun time for us. She was more playful, and I would read the newspaper. Once, she took the sports section out of the large Sunday paper and watched while I rifled through each section, cursing that they left out the section I wanted. She laughed aloud after revealing that she'd had it all along. This morning was a long way from fun or relaxing.

As I walked toward the coffee pot for a refill, she started toward the refrigerator for a bottle of water. Crossing paths, we awkwardly stepped around each other without speaking, got what we needed, and went back to our corners like boxers retreating at round's end. After we'd sat silently at opposite ends of the living room for several minutes, I couldn't take it anymore and spoke.

"This is not us, Trish, not the way we've always handled problems."

"No, but I need time, so let's just leave it alone for now."

"OK. I understand why you need that, but I don't think that silence is the answer to anything. We need to at least talk about what we're both thinking right now, so we're not walking on eggshells and avoiding each other, as though we haven't had thirty years together."

I got up and anxiously paced back and forth, gesturing as if admitting defeat.

"Just what do you expect me to do?" Trish asked.

"I don't expect anything. Call me a son of a bitch, kick me in the groin, slap my face, just don't shut me out right now. I need to know how you feel."

"How I feel? Hurt, confused, shocked. How would you feel if I came home and told you the same?" she replied.

"I'd feel just like you do right now."

"Yes, and you'd be wondering what I was going to do next and where this marriage is headed."

"Exactly why we need to talk. I told you last night that I wouldn't pursue this if it was going to destroy us," I said.

"Right. That's what you say now, but you've never been through anything like this. How can you know where it takes you? Not pursue it! It's impossible for me to believe that we can just forget this ever happened or that you can just move on from here, knowing that you needed help, found it, then let go of it."

"There's so much I don't know yet, but what I do know is that I love you more than anything in this world. Whatever I do to ease my own pain, to become my real self, would be cancelled out and meaningless without you by my side. Why would I try to become something else if I'm nothing without you?" I said.

Through our front window, I saw school kids playing as they waited for the morning bus. When I looked back, Trish had gotten up and moved toward the stairs.

"We have lots to talk about, and we will. We have a lot to think about before we do, so let's just think about things today and talk later. Does that work for you?" Trish said.

"Fair enough. I can wait until you're ready," I said.

"That's going to take time."

"Just so we keep talking, that's all I ask," I replied.

Chapter Nineteen: Breaking Silence

"You go ahead, honey; I'll use the downstairs bathroom," I said.

It had been three days since my revelation, and Trish and I had hardly spoken. Now, outside of the bathroom, we danced around each other like awkward strangers. This had to change.

"No, you go ahead," Trish said, "I'll go downstairs."

I found myself bowing and extending my left arm towards the bathroom.

"After you, madame, I insist!" I did my best French accent, hoping some humor would help.

When Trish laughed, I felt relieved, and my anxiety disappeared.

"Here's an idea, Trish, let's get out of the house and take in a late morning movie. We need to do something together today."

I was hoping we could talk more easily if we did something we'd always enjoyed together. She didn't reply immediately and left a very long, awkward moment of silence. Maybe I was moving this along too fast.

"Sounds like a plan," Trish said.

I was relieved. We had taken the difficult first step towards opening the lines of communication in the way we've been solving our problems for years: relaxed and open.

Walking into our favorite theater was always a treat. The sound of popcorn popping greeted us in the lobby, and the smell guided us to the concessions. Each theater in the Palms was decorated with different movie paraphernalia. Our movie selection was on Ancient Egypt. Among pyramids, sphinxes, mummies, and giant posters from Cleopatra and other Egyptian-themed movies, we were immediately transported.

This is just what we need, I thought. Our love for movies was the common ground we could build on.

After a light-hearted rom-com, Trish seemed relaxed and cheerful in the passenger's seat of the car. I began the conversation that broke the ice.

"OK, so we've had time to think for a few days. Are we ready to talk about it?"

Trish hesitated, looking down at her hands, then adjusted her outside mirror. "Yes, but damn it, there's so much going through my mind, I don't know where to begin," she replied.

"That's understandable. What if I just ask you a question to get it going?"

"Fair enough," she said.

"I know that I'm worried about tons of things, and you must be too. What worries you the most?"

Trish turned her head and looked towards me as I focused on the traffic ahead.

"That I'm losing you. I don't know what this means to our marriage. Are you going to leave me for a man as soon as you become a woman? How are we defined? How do I introduce you now? Are you my wife or spouse or what? It's all so confusing!"

I felt overwhelmed and guilty at the same time. I'd put her in a place of uncertainty and emotional agony. I was anxious to reassure her that those issues were not going to be a problem for us.

"Those are huge concerns for you, and I understand. First, gender identity and sexuality are two separate things. I've always been attracted to women; men don't interest me in the least."

Gazing out the passenger window, Trish responded, "You say that now, and I'm sure it's true, but you've never physically been female. How do you know for certain what emotional changes come along with taking hormones and altering your body?"

I drove the last few blocks home while thinking about the question. Pulling into our tuck-under garage, I took her hand in mine.

"I don't, Trish, but there are things I am absolute about. I absolutely love you and have for more than thirty years. Nothing is going to change that. I'm not sure how far I need to go with the physical changes, but whatever I do wouldn't be powerful enough to change the way I feel about you. You *are* my life, and I will never be interested in anyone else."

Trish was quiet for a long moment as we got out of the car.

"I know that you believe what you're saying right now, but neither of us knows where this could go."

Stepping closer, I placed both hands on her shoulders and moved in closer.

"That is true, but when I made the promise to love you forever, I meant it. I will make you another promise right now. We will go through this together, and I will NOT make any decisions on my own when it comes to transitioning, surgery, or anything else. I won't do this without you."

Trish put her arms around me, and we embraced. Tears ran down her cheeks, and I began to cry as I felt her tears on my face.

"I love you, too! We have to find our way through this together," Trish said.

We stepped into the house and settled into the white leather swivel chairs in the living room.

Composing herself, Trish asked, "So we didn't talk about what concerns you the most."

I didn't have to think about my answer. It had been foremost in my mind since I started therapy.

"I don't want to lose you, Trish. That's my number one fear. You married a man, and now you'll have a woman. I'm worried you're going to find another man, and I wouldn't blame you. This isn't what you signed up for."

Trish swiveled back and forth, relieving the tense energy brought on by our talk.

"That's not going to happen either!" Trish said. "I don't need a man in my life, but you're right, I did marry one. Let me ask you, how far do you plan to go with this?"

"What do you mean by how far?"

"I mean, do your plans include surgery and living as a woman?"

I wasn't sure what to say. I felt like she deserved an answer, but was asking a premature question. I just didn't have enough information yet. I swiveled my chair full circle, got up, and walked around the room to clear my head.

"I don't know yet. It's too early in the process. I need more therapy and time to fully understand what I need to do. I don't see how any physical changes are possible until I retire."

"Why wait until you retire? Isn't that prolonging the agony?" Trish asked.

She was absolutely right. My choice would've been to go full speed ahead immediately, but that would not be wise. I'd been down and out too many times in my life, and that was its own brand of agony. I wouldn't risk financial ruin.

"It's the business I'm in. It's male-dominant to the extreme and not very socially progressive. I would not last very long in my business if I made the change."

"How do you know that for sure?"

I was not. I could only go by my personal experiences with those I was dealing with at the time. I couldn't condemn an entire industry, because I *had* worked with some reasonable, kind people. The problem with leaping into the unknown is that you must consider worst-case scenarios. You can't think bad things could possibly happen; you must assume they will.

"Trust me, I'm a hundred percent sure of one major problem that would occur."

Trish got up, walked across the room, and grabbed a soda from the fridge.

"You want one of these?"

"Sure, thanks."

"What major problem are you so sure of?" Trish asked.

"The largest customer I have buys a million dollars a year in product from us, and in turn, I sell their products to my United States customers. I have two streams of income with them that we can't afford to lose."

"I don't get why you're sure you'll lose them."

"Remember, the owner comes down from Canada to travel with me, making sales calls. You learn a lot about someone when you travel by car for a week, have every meal together, and have tons of time to talk. He was talking about his troubles finding quality people to fill open jobs. He's gone through several interviews and rejected most candidates."

"What's so bad about that?"

"It's *why* he rejected them. If they had long hair, tattoos, piercings of any kind, or were different in any way, he considered them to be of weak character and ruled them out. So, what chance do you think I'd have if he knew anything about what I am?" I said.

Trish took a gulp of her soda. "I think it would be over immediately. About how much of your total business would that be?" she asked.

"I'd have to guess about 70 percent of total sales."

Trish got out of her chair and walked towards me. "That much? I didn't know you had so much with one account."

I thought of how much time I'd devoted to this customer and supplier over 20 years. Was I being too protective? They had consumed most of my time and energy over those years, and I didn't have time to pursue other accounts. The money was great, but the risk of having everything in one account was sky high. Had I fallen back into my lifelong habit of living to satisfy everyone else's image of what I should be? Maybe it was time to stop worrying about them and focus on what's right for our well-being, my well-being.

Sitting down again, Trish looked puzzled. "You've held this inside your entire life, discovered the truth, and now you have to hide it away again?"

"Yes, but it's the only option for us right now. I can't do what I feel, I can't put everything we've worked for at risk."

"But haven't you talked with your therapist regarding business issues?"

"I have, Trish, but it's complicated. She has clients in the same circumstances. They are transitioning slowly, less visibly."

"I don't even know what that means!" Trish said, now exasperated.

"I'm not sure I do either, but from what I understand, they start on female hormones so they can feel congruent in mind and body. The visual changes are minimal, but it is the first step required for anyone transitioning. Dr. Deb follows procedural guidelines."

"Ok," Trish said, "as a nurse, I see the importance of following guidelines when it comes to standards of care. What's the first step?"

"Dr. Deb would refer me to a physician for evaluation to determine if I should begin HRT, hormone replacement therapy."

"You sound like you have confidence in Doctor Deb's opinion."

"She's knowledgeable and has helped over three hundred patients transition. I trust her completely."

Trish paused for a moment. "What's the next step for us?"

"Dr. Deb suggests you come to a session with me. She can meet with you first, then see us together."

Trish's body language showed fluent speaking tension. I could see her tighten up.

"I'm not sure I want to do that. What does that accomplish?" she said.

This was a good time for me to bring Trish's training up and help her understand that she WAS an important part of this. Not only as my wife, but as someone who could bring a different perspective into the room.

"She could answer questions you have about her qualifications and how she has helped me to this point. I'm sure you want to be a part of this process, and I think your mental health background would be of benefit to us."

"Those would be the top two. I'm sure I will have many more. When would you want to do this?"

"As soon as possible. I'll let her know that you'll be coming to my next appointment."

"OK, but I'm going to do this one time only. I think it's more important for you to have time with her alone."

"Fair enough, I'm happy you're open to seeing her. I think you'll be impressed."

"We'll see about that," Trish said as she left the room, "there's only one way for me to find out."

Her skepticism concerned me, but it was understandable. I could only hope she approached our meeting as the open-minded woman I'd always known her to be. But as she said, there would be only one way to find out.

Chapter Twenty: Doctor Deb Revisited

"We're ready for you to join us, Michael," Dr. Deb said as she swung her office door open. I'd been waiting in the outer office for 45 minutes while Trish and the doctor had a private conversation. We'd agreed that Trish would have the opportunity to ask questions while I was not in the room, and Dr. Deb could get to know more about her. We'd also settled on addressing me by my male name and pronouns until we were comfortable with moving towards transition.

Trish's body language was in full defensive mode. Sitting upright, arms folded across her chest, and legs crossed, she seemed tense.

"Are you OK?" I asked.

"Yes, I'm fine," she replied.

I swallowed hard. If Trish asked how her hair looked and I said "fine," she'd reply, "Really? Fine? Just fine?" Then she'd redo her hair completely and be upset with me. I'd learned to say "wonderful" instead.

"We did have a good discussion," Dr. Deb said. "We agreed on which things the three of us can talk about together. The rest will remain privileged between Trish and me."

That threw me off a little. What wasn't I supposed to know? But it was fair that Trish was protected by the same doctor–patient privilege I was afforded.

"Where do we all begin?" I said.

Dr. Deb settled into her swivel chair and swung around to face us. "I'd like to start by clarifying something. Trish asked a particularly important question about the standards of care I live by and what guidelines I follow. I can see her background in mental health is going to be helpful here."

Trish relaxed after that comment and eased back in her chair. She felt included now. That was always important to her, and I tried to be aware of it.

"I didn't answer Trish then because I wanted you to hear this as well, Michael. It's important for you to know."

She rolled her chair a little closer to us. "When I am counseling anyone about gender dysphoria, I strictly follow the standards of care guidelines set forth by the World Professional Association for Transgender Health, also known as WPATH."

"What professions are they affiliated with?" Trish asked.

"They consist of a wide range of medical doctors, surgeons, therapists, medical research scientists, and associated caregivers who are dedicated to the health and well-being of the transgender community worldwide. They have established requirements for care and the process of transitioning. I would never recommend you to anyone or suggest any procedure that is not within those guidelines," Dr. Deb said.

"That's reassuring," I said. "Can you give us an example of how that works?"

Dr. Deb leaned forward. "Yes. Let's assume you decide to begin transitioning. Typically, I begin by recommending you to a doctor I have used many times. He would be your first step in the WPATH process. He has treated many transgender patients of mine. He would examine and interview you to determine if you are a candidate for HRT, or hormone replacement therapy, which is the first stage of transition."

These were details Dr. Deb and I had discussed in detail previously. I wanted to make sure Trish heard them from the source.

"How would that affect me, and would changes be visible?" I asked.

"Nothing very dramatic in the first year," Dr. Deb replied. "Your skin will soften over time, you'll lose muscle mass, and small breasts will develop over a longer period of time."

"Ok, what about facial hair, and my voice?" I asked.

"Unfortunately, facial hair is very stubborn. You'll have to undergo several hundred hours of electrolysis to remove it completely. For a male-to-female transition, you're out of luck on the voice, also. The voice will not change, because the male vocal cords remain the same."

"That sounds like a long, painful process for facial hair removal," Trish said.

"It is, and it's expensive too," Dr. Deb replied.

"So, can anything be done about the voice?" I said. "I've seen transwomen on television who have very feminine voices."

"Everyone is different," Dr. Deb said. "Some have higher voices to begin with, or they alter their voice through lessons or coaching."

"Doesn't sound like I have much chance; I have little vocal control. Ask Trish, she's heard me sing!" I joked. "But seriously, Dr. Deb, how would the female hormones affect me emotionally?"

"Great question. Estrogen will alter your physiology after taking it for a while. That will cause emotional changes for certain. The number one thing I hear from my patients is that they feel congruent within their mind/body and are much more relaxed and comfortable in their own skin."

"How does that interact with the existing testosterone?" Trish asked.

Dr. Deb looked surprised. "You *do* have great questions, Trish, and they're truly relevant to what I'm about to say."

"Hey, I'm trying!" Trish laughed.

Dr. Deb continued. "Michael would be prescribed spironolactone as a hormone blocker to reduce the amount of testosterone in the body, allowing the female hormones to become dominant."

"How long would that treatment continue?" I asked.

"You would be on estrogen indefinitely. We don't like to have anyone on spironolactone for more than a year. It would be stopped just before any procedure that permanently halts the body's production of testosterone."

Trish shifted in her chair, looking uncomfortable again. "What are the procedures you're talking about?"

Dr. Deb noticed Trish's anxiety. "We can move on to another subject if you like, Trish. This is all in the context of the question regarding procedural guidelines."

Trish took a deep breath, relaxed, and said, "That's OK, we should hear this. It's just for information purposes at this point."

"That's all it is," I said.

Dr. Deb got out of her chair, walked across the room, and filled her water glass. "Anyone like some?"

"No, thanks," we both replied.

Sitting back in her chair, she turned to Trish.

"I must tell you, Trish. I admire your courage. You are a brave woman. These are difficult conversations to have, so deeply personal and life-altering. So many spouses have refused to come in and talk together or make any attempt to understand. This can be a deal breaker in a marriage. Michael has been talking about you for weeks now, and meeting you confirms the positive things I've been hearing."

Trish looked at ease once again, shifting her body back in her chair.

"Thanks," she said, "but it's not bravery so much as it is love and concern. If I didn't care about him so much, I wouldn't be here."

Dr. Deb continued. "What strikes me the most is the strength of the relationship and the communication skills you have together. That's so vital to surviving any crisis."

"We've had that since we met. We've survived lots of challenging times," I said.

"And it's going to be important to keep that in the days to come," said Dr. Deb. "As for your question, the option chosen depends on the individual's wants and needs. Some choose an orchiectomy, which is testicular removal through surgery. This eliminates the production of testosterone entirely and allows for the estrogen to take over."

Half joking, I crossed my legs together tightly. Grimacing, I said, "And just what are the other options?"

"Again, it depends on what you personally need to consider transition complete. There are those who feel the need for a complete vaginoplasty, which removes all male genitalia and surgically forms a vagina. Others chose orchiectomy only. That would all be up to you."

Trish and I hadn't talked about any surgical procedures. It had been just a few weeks since I informed her of my therapy sessions and what was revealed. I thought this was moving too fast, and I should protect her from becoming overwhelmed.

"We get the picture, Dr. Deb. That's probably enough on procedures for now," I said.

"Sure. I just want you to understand that these procedures have proven to be effective and are required to take place in order, but there are options. The choices are yours. Is that enough information for you, too, Trish?"

"Absolutely, and thanks for explaining all of that," Trish replied.

Dr. Deb paused for a moment as she looked at the notebook on her lap. She flipped through the pages a few times, read for a minute, then said, "Trish, when we talked alone, I asked how long you've been together, and you mentioned you were approaching your thirtieth anniversary. You also said you guys have had a very natural connection from the beginning."

"Yes, I did say that, and it is true," Trish said.

"Great, do you mind if I ask what qualities attracted you? What impressed you about Michael that drew you together?"

"No, I don't mind. He's always been kind, gentle, and loving. He cares about others and isn't afraid to show emotions or share feelings. Then there's that sense of humor that's always had a way of making me laugh when I'm upset or feeling down."

"Yes, and I'm humble too!" I said.

"Interesting." Dr Deb nodded. "So, while these traits aren't exclusively female, don't you think these are considered to be more feminine qualities?"

"Yes, I suppose most men would shy away from being identified with feminine traits," Trish replied.

"Undoubtedly. So, let me ask you, Trish. Do you think that all these qualities you love about Michael will be anything but enhanced by him becoming a complete person, free of anxiety and inner turmoil?"

Trish considered that for a moment. "No, I would imagine he would be happier and healthier emotionally. I want him to be happy. It's figuring out how we live with it together."

I was moved by Dr. Deb's question, even more so by Trish's reply. I grabbed the Kleenex on the table next to me and dried my eyes before the tears could stream down my cheeks. I reached for Trish's hand.

"I know I would be happier, but not without you. I never dreamed I could become my true self. Yes, I would continue to have the same traits, only I will become a better, more complete version of myself."

"That's a great way to look at it, Michael," Dr. Deb said.

Trish placed her hand on top of mine and turned towards me. "I know you truly mean what you say, but neither of us knows what's ahead. This is uncharted territory."

Dr. Deb watched us. "Considering what I've seen from you two, and everything I know about you, I believe you will make this work. I have good instincts, and I can see you care deeply about each other. Trish, you care enough to have come here, and Michael cares so much that he said he wouldn't do this without you. I've had husbands tell me they didn't care what their wives thought, they were moving ahead with or without them. Neither of you is a selfish person. That is key to staying together."

"That's true," Trish said. "We also have our faith to draw from. We passionately believe God never gives us more than we can handle. Even if we don't see it at the time, we end up right where we're supposed to be."

"As the daughter of a minister, and as one who has studied theology, I couldn't agree more," Dr. Deb said.

"I wasn't aware of that!" Trish said.

"Yes, it was a strong part of my educational experience."

I could tell Trish was impressed with the scope of Doctor Deb's background.

"Interesting. I do have another question," Trish said. "How did you reach the conclusion of gender dysphoria?"

"I'm happy you asked," Dr. Deb replied. "I once said I would never *tell* Michael what he is, but my diagnosis would be key in determining gender dysphoria. I don't have a crystal ball to look into. I'm only human, but I can apply my years of expertise to create a person's profile, past and present. We've explored everything from childhood to the present day. There are several recurring emotional red flags, and Michael raised every one of them. Not only the constant longing to dress and express a female persona, but his description of 'feeling right with the world' in every single instance since childhood when dressed feminine, followed by a sense of loss when returning to male attire. I think it's safe to say that Michael is transgendered."

Trish sat quietly for a moment, once again absorbing the reality of the diagnosis.

"Ok, that sounds very detailed and complete," she said.

Feeling guilty again, I thought I needed to add a few words.

"It wasn't a snap decision by any stretch of the imagination. I struggled with myself to let the truth out," I said.

Dr. Deb paged through her notebook, slowing the pace of the conversation as she prepared to sum it up... beautifully.

"You've wrestled with your conscience since our first session. You've held onto this so tightly for so many years. Your trouble is letting your defense mechanism down. Let me reassure you, no one has ever come through this door until the exact moment they were meant to. You've lived your life to this point the way you were 'supposed to'. You've been there and remained strong for the sake of others. You are here now because it is your time to become yourself, *exactly* your time."

"Wow, very well put," I said.

"That is a positive way to see it," Trish added.

"What's the next step? Where do we go from here?" I said.

"I recommend you continue with our sessions. There are so many things to consider, and I will be happy to guide you through them. Trish, you're welcome to come anytime you need to, and I thank you for coming today. You've been a huge help in understanding the dynamics of this relationship."

"Thank you, Dr. Deb. It's been enlightening for me too; I've learned a lot today," Trish replied. "We've got plenty to talk about at home, but I still don't understand where we're going from this point. We do have business relationships to be concerned about. Not everyone will be agreeable."

"I think we need to begin carefully, but we do need to get started. I could see starting hormones and doing electrolysis. Knowing I'm taking steps, however small they may be, towards becoming myself would be huge for me," I said.

"Exactly. It's time to get moving," Trish added.

I was impressed with how far Trish had come since agreeing to see the doctor with me. I don't know what their private talk involved or what changed her outlook, but she seemed ready to move ahead with everything. Given her background, I suspected she needed to hear the clinical explanation directly from the doctor.

"That's the question, isn't it?" Dr. Deb said. "In this situation, I would suggest you take a trip somewhere you feel safe with Michael dressed and living as a woman, maybe for a week or so. It's an effective way to assess the comfort level of being 'out' publicly and would give '*her*' time to explore."

"That's a great idea!" I said, knowing I would love it.

I was certain I knew just the place to go.

Chapter Twenty-one: Taking Time Out

———————— • ————————

"I need time alone, and you need to take this trip by yourself," Trish said emphatically.

"Dr. Deb suggested we do this together," I replied.

"*Suggested* is the keyword. She didn't say we had to," Trish replied. "I have to sort out everything I've learned in the last several weeks, and I don't think your being here will help. I can't gather my thoughts without some time alone."

I knew Trish was right, but I was hurt by the idea that she needed to be away from me. We'd been separated when I was out of town on business, but we'd never isolated for purposes of soul-searching.

I stood up and moved closer, lowering my voice.

"You can't seriously believe that I'm going to Wilton Manors by myself, leaving you here worrying about me, about us?"

"Yes, I do!" Trish responded. "It's the only way for both of us to figure out where we're headed. Take all of your women's outfits, makeup, wigs, everything you need to live for five days or so, and get a true feeling of what this could be like for you. Go out to dinner with your friends, have a few drinks, whatever. It'll be good for you."

"Yeah, the freedom to be out publicly as myself would be incredible, but I wouldn't be able to stop feeling selfish long enough to enjoy myself. I'd be in sunny Florida with friends while you'd be home alone in the cold, gray Illinois winter."

Trish stood up from her chair. "Jake, let's go outside." Jake bolted to her with a leash in his mouth.

"Wait a minute, we're not done talking here," I said.

"I am, until I take a walk and you think for a few minutes about why we're having this conversation," Trish said, as she hurried out the door with Jake.

I was upset Trish had walked away before I finished talking, but it allowed me time to cool down and think. I owed her time alone, if that's what she wanted. After all, this began with my time alone while she was in Florida, and I understood why she needed solitude.

I began to think about how being by myself might work. I wouldn't have to be worried about Trish feeling left out if I were spending all of my time with my friends. I could spend time alone shopping, dining, going to the museum, or whatever struck me at the moment. I enjoyed doing all of these things with Trish, but this could be helpful in developing a sense of confidence on my own, as a woman. I could see what it felt like to do things instinctively.

After about twenty minutes, the patio door opened, and Jake ran to his water bowl while Trish walked into the kitchen.

I followed behind her. "OK, Trish, you're right," I said.

"My favorite phrase," she replied. "About what?"

"I've laid a lot on your shoulders this last month, and I need to allow you time to sort it out. This should be a time for both of us to discover on our own just what we need as individuals in our new lives. We're both affected by this, and I should allow you just as much space to think things through," I said.

"I'm glad you see that!" she said.

"It took a minute, but I understand the wisdom in going alone."

"Alright. Tell me what you're thinking then."

"It would be easier if you were with me. I'd be in my comfort zone with you by my side. By myself, I'd be isolated. I'd feel the positive and negative aspects of socializing as a woman. I wouldn't have you there as a buffer to fall back on if things get uncomfortable. I'd be working without a net and could learn quickly whether or not I have the courage to present myself full-time as female."

"Wow," Trish replied, "I can't say I thought it out exactly like that, but it makes a lot of sense. You can't base everything on one outing, but it'll give you an idea of what you're facing in the real world."

"That's true. I think it's the reasoning behind Doctor Deb's suggestion to take this trip," I replied.

I appreciated that Trish needed time to get an unobstructed view of the stage being set for our new lives together. What part would she play? Could she be herself, or would she have to adapt to an entirely improvised, unforeseen role?

This would be the first time since my revelation that we would have an extended amount of time alone. We would both be exploring possibilities that neither one of us thought we'd be facing in all of our years together. Our futures would be tied to how we individually viewed our time apart. Uncharted waters do not often result in smooth sailing. The results would be life-changing, either way.

Chapter Twenty-Two:
Back on the Boulevard

"Hi Ed! How're you doing?" I said as I opened the front door of the main check-in cottage at our usual resort.

"Hey, so great to see you, Mike! I was so happy to find out you were coming to visit us again. Is Trish out in the car?"

"No, I'm here on my own for five nights, and I have some big news to tell you."

Ed looked concerned. "Is everything OK with you guys?"

"Sure, we just needed some time apart, which brings me to my news."

"Now I am intrigued," Ed replied. "What's going on?"

Ed poured me a shot of tequila. He was always good at remembering what his regular guests liked to drink and quick to accommodate.

"I have some freshly baked cookies if you'd like," Ed said as he handed me my shot.

"No thanks, it's a little early in the day for cookies," I joked as I downed my tequila.

We both laughed.

"So, tell me your news."

"Well, Ed, you've known for as long as we've been coming here on Halloween, I've always dressed as a woman."

"Yeah, I did notice how much you enjoy yourself, and that's what we're here for."

"I know, it's what I love about your place, and Wilton Manors," I replied. "Well, a few days after last year's three-day marathon, I was so empty inside and conflicted. I felt like I needed answers, so I began seeing a therapist who specializes in gender-related issues. Working together, we determined that I am transgender."

Ed got out of his chair, walked over, and gave me a huge hug. "That's so wonderful. You've found yourself! I am so happy for you, my friend. We'll have to go out and celebrate while you're here."

I wasn't surprised how quickly he accepted what I just told him. As a gay young man growing up in Puerto Rico, Ed had faced many challenges. His experiences had made him empathetic.

"Thanks, Ed, I knew that I could count on your support."

"Absolutely!" Ed replied.

The smile left his face, and he looked concerned again. "But what about Trish, is she ok with this, is that why she's not here?"

"It's a lot for her," I replied. "We're doing everything we can to stay together. We still love each other, and we're going to work through this. I'm here by myself because part of my therapy is to live as a woman when I can. I'll see what challenges I face and whether or not I can handle the changes."

"That makes good sense. So, Trish is OK with you coming by yourself?"

"It was her idea. She needs time alone to think, and I have to do this on my own if I'm going to learn anything. It works out for both of us."

"That's what I love about you guys. You're not afraid to do what's best for each other," Ed replied.

Ed walked around his desk to the keys hanging on the wall, tossing one over. "Let's get you settled in your cottage. By the way, what are we going to call you now? I'm sure you don't want to be known as Mike."

"Thanks for asking. I've recently decided on Isabella. My mom's name was Isabel, and that honors her, but I also love the name Bella, so I prefer to be called Bella."

"I love it," Ed replied. "OK, Bella, let's go!"

Later that evening, I thought I'd go check out the clubs on Wilton Boulevard, have a drink, and test my comfort level. Getting ready, I realized I didn't have any casual evening clothes. I had a few pairs of jeans and T-shirts, but they weren't fit for clubbing. I would rather be overdressed than under. I slipped into an Ultrasuede cocktail dress trimmed with tiers of fringe. It was the least conspicuous dress I had with me. What the hell was I thinking? This wasn't Halloween.

I walked a few blocks unnoticed, then a group of younger men brushed close by me, and I almost fell off the sidewalk, avoiding a collision.

I kept walking and heard one of them say, "Is that your prom dress, honey?" in a very catty tone. They all had a good laugh at my expense.

Still, I was relieved it wasn't a group of young straight men. I might have experienced more than an insult. Nonetheless, I felt disrespected. No one had verbally insulted me here before. It caught me off guard. I'm usually pretty quick to return jabs, but I let it go. If they had a problem, they owned it. I was going to enjoy my first night "out."

I went from club to club in Wilton. No one seemed very friendly. I began to feel out of place and uncomfortable. I sat at the bar in most clubs, trying to strike up a conversation, but was completely ignored. Not even the bartenders were friendly. I sensed I was not welcome.

What a contrast this was to the party atmosphere I'd experienced in the past! I didn't expect things to be the same as on a festival night, but this crowd appeared to be focused on one thing. This had more of a "meat market" atmosphere than I recalled.

I finished my drink and went back to my cottage to call Trish and say goodnight.

"Hi honey, how are you doing?"

She was silent for a moment, then replied, "I'm OK. How are things going?"

She sounded different, aloof and distant.

"Everything good there, are you alright?" I asked.

"Yeah, I'm just tired and getting ready for bed. I've had a long day," she replied.

"I'm sorry, long how? What happened?" I had a sense that she was beginning to have second thoughts about us staying together.

"Nothing. Don't worry about me, what did you do tonight?" she asked.

"I walked down to the clubs, had a drink, not very welcoming or friendly people out tonight."

"That's too bad. Maybe you should see if Ed wants to go out tomorrow."

"I was planning on stopping by the resort office tomorrow and seeing if he does."

As we talked, I was struck by the frailty in her voice. Was she feeling abandoned? Sadness rose within me as I realized how difficult this journey into transition was going to be for both of us, but especially for Trish. I was certain to have plenty of difficulties, but I would be able to deal with whatever came along, knowing that I was gaining the freedom of being my true self at last.

Trish would be losing her husband of 30 years. She'd have to deal with the social stigma involved in living with me, being my wife and partner. What would her friends think? How would she be treated by people in our community? Would she have to worry every time we left the house? I fully realized the burden I was placing on her, and I felt guilty.

"I'm going to bed now, so love you and goodnight," Trish said, ending our brief conversation.

"I miss you," I said, but I could tell by her voice she was somewhere I couldn't reach.

The next morning, I awoke remembering the sting of the young men's words on the sidewalk. I needed to find more appropriate clothes. I went shopping the minute the stores opened. I purchased a variety of skirts, tops, and slacks. They were casual to dressy and would cover any occasion for the week. I returned to my room, threw on a denim skirt, a sleeveless print top, and felt more confident in my appearance. I walked over to the main check-in office, where Ed introduced me to two gentlemen seated in the waiting area.

"Bella, come in and meet my guests Victor and Steve. They are staying here until they close on a house they just bought in the neighborhood."

We exchanged greetings and small talk for a few minutes and hit it off quickly. Ed asked how my first night went, and I told them the problem I was having with being ignored.

"Bella is transitioning to female, and this is her coming out week," Ed said.

"Wonderful!" Victor chimed in.

"But Bella, you are going to the wrong clubs!" Ed said in a mock-scolding way. "These clubs around here have much younger crowds. Things have changed; it's all about the quick hook-ups now."

"Yeah, I got that impression last night. What would you suggest, Ed?"

"You should go to the drag clubs. People go there to have fun. The atmosphere is friendly, and the shows are great."

"That sounds like fun," Steve said.

"I know where you need to go, you have to check out LIPS! It is not a bar, it's a drag dinner theatre with celebrity impersonators. The crowd is a cross-section of people, straight, gay, young, and old. Lots of ladies have their bachelorette parties there. It's a real lively place," Ed said.

"Is it mostly groups?" I asked.

"Not all big groups, but I think you need more than one to reserve a table," Ed replied.

Steve stood up and joined in. "You know what would be fun? Why don't the four of us go together and we'll celebrate Bella's big news!"

I was so relieved to hear that. What a great idea. I wouldn't have to go alone, and now I had two new friends. It was a beautiful gesture.

"The four of us will go then!" I exclaimed.

I had a few days before our reservation and spent my time exploring more of Fort Lauderdale. I went to the Galleria Shops, a very popular upscale mall. I was excited about our night out and wanted just the right dress. I found a classy silver cocktail dress for the occasion and was pleased with the fit and how I looked.

I had lunch alone at a sidewalk cafe in front of Neiman Marcus, and felt people were staring at me. I'm sure that some were, but I didn't care. I was enjoying myself too much to worry about them. I told myself to get used to it;

this would be one of the things I'd have to learn to deal with.

I was also learning about my own misconceptions. Maybe they weren't staring at me. Maybe it was my imagination, and I was projecting my inner fear of being judged or rejected. I couldn't know for sure. Wouldn't I enjoy the day more if I simply didn't speculate? This trip was becoming a very interesting experiment in human behavior, both mine and the people I encountered.

On the day of our group outing to the club, the parking lot at LIPS was filling with shuttle vans from area retirement communities and hotels. A group of young women was waiting for the rest of their party to arrive before going in. Entering, I could see there was a large and diverse crowd.

Once we were seated, a stunning brunette server approached the table. She was shimmering and delightful-looking in her candy-colored outfit. She portrayed a beautiful likeness of Katy Perry in her "California Gurls" video.

"Anyone in this group having a birthday today or celebrating something special?" she asked.

"Yes! We're celebrating the beginning of Bella's new life as a woman; she's starting her transition," Ed said, putting his arm on my shoulder.

"Wow, congratulations, honey!" Katy said, taking our drink order, then quickly disappearing into the back room.

She returned a few minutes later with our drinks. "Bella, honey, do you have any problem going up on stage tonight?"

Her question threw me off. "I guess not, I mean, I don't have stage fright. I'm not shy in front of crowds. Why?"

"Our Master of Ceremonies-slash-Hostess-slash-Queen of the Divas thinks what you're doing is very special and would love to do a toast to celebrate you."

"I can't refuse a sweet gesture like that. Sure, I'd love to."

"Super. After the birthday announcements, she'll introduce you, and I'll escort you up."

I was surprised. I hadn't expected any special attention or treatment. It made me feel special to have the outside world recognize the importance of this week for me. After each performer did their individual act, the MC returned.

"We are not done yet, folks," she said after she'd wished an older man happy birthday and blown kisses to a bachelorette. "We have someone special with us tonight who is celebrating a magnificent event in her life."

Just then, our Katy Perry was back, extending her hand to me. "C'mon, Bella, let's walk up together," she said in a whisper.

Walking up to the stage, I was nervous I might fall off my heels. What was I getting myself into?

I relaxed as I made it to the stage and our MC spoke. "Ladies and Gentlemen, please give a big LIPS welcome to MISS BELLA!"

She put her arm around my shoulders and put the microphone in my face while the crowd gave me a warm round of applause. I was getting emotional and did my best to keep it together.

"I'll bet you didn't expect this when you left the house tonight, Bella!"

"No, I'd have dressed better if I did," I replied.

"You look pretty damn good to me, girl; would you share with us what you're celebrating?"

"Yes. We're here to celebrate my coming out as a transwoman and the beginning of my transition to female."

"That is fantastic!" she exclaimed as the audience erupted in loud applause. "And it is so brave. Can I ask how old you are?"

"No," I laughed.

"Oh, I see, darling, never ask a lady her age."

"Really, not a problem, I'm 63."

"Oh my god, you don't look a day over 62 and a half. But all kidding aside, Bella, GOOD FOR YOU!"

"Thank you, I'm very happy!" I said.

"Well, we salute you. You do realize that by coming up here, you must now be crowned 'Diva of the Day' and fully consume our signature drink — the 'Pick the Diva Off the Floor.'" She placed a plastic tiara on my head and handed me a large, colorful drink.

"I'd be honored to do that," I said.

"Let's raise our glasses to Bella, everyone. We wish you the best of everything, and all the happiness you deserve in your new life."

I downed my drink as the crowd cheered me on and applauded. I placed my hands on my face, feigning a pageant winner's surprise as she was crowned Miss America. I got another good laugh from the crowd, but my tears were real. The Shania Twain song, "Man, I Feel Like a Woman," began playing as I walked back to our table.

I was elated and overwhelmed with emotion. I felt such love and affection from the entire room. I didn't believe it was possible to receive this much acceptance. What a difference a few days can make.

My friends stood up and hugged me before I sat.

"You were fabulous up there, Bella!" Ed said.

"Yes! That was so cool," Victor added.

"I can't help it; I'm going to cry. I am over the moon right now. I feel like I've been formally introduced and accepted as a woman tonight," I said.

"In my culture, we celebrate a young girl's entry to womanhood with a Quinceañera. This is your Quinceañera, Bella!" Ed said.

Later, as we filed from the building, I was met with encouragement and pats on the back. As I got to our car, a very small, frail, elderly woman grabbed my hand and held onto it. She looked at me seriously and said, "Don't ever let anyone tell you that you can't be exactly who you are!"

I was so touched, I started to tear up again. I put my free hand on top of hers.

"Thank you so much. I won't, and I will always remember your advice."

She smiled, turned, and walked away.

Back at the cottage, I packed my bags and prepared for tomorrow morning's flight home. When I called Trish, she seemed to be in a better frame of mind.

I didn't want to be over-exuberant about my evening, but I did tell her about the wonderful moments. She was happy for me and said, "See, that's why you went by yourself. It was a success."

"It was a breakthrough. I know it was a friendly environment, but if a room full of strangers can accept me, there's hope," I replied.

"Good for you! I've had a few breakthroughs of my own in the last few days. I've had lots of time to think about things. I've talked to some friends, and I've done some productive research. I've learned something important," Trish said.

"That's great. What did you learn about?"

"I don't think I want to talk about it on the phone. I'd rather wait until I see you in person to give you all the details."

Didn't want to talk about it on the phone? I did not like the sound of that. She had never had a problem sharing over the phone, so why now? If what she learned was good news, I knew she'd be anxious to tell me. Otherwise, she would likely wait to tell me in person. Talked to friends? That could mean anything. Sometimes friends take one side of the argument only and influence an important decision without knowing all the facts. I was worried and wanted to be home as soon as possible.

Chapter Twenty-Three: Restless at the Starting Gate

"You upstairs, Trish?" I put my bags down in the hallway. I'd worried the entire trip home about the epiphany she'd had while I was in Florida. The roles had been reversed. Just a few months ago, I stayed home while Trish was in Florida, and I revealed something life-changing upon her return. I didn't know if this would be good or bad news for our future together. I assumed I knew her well enough to trust that she would remain with me in my transition, but then again, she couldn't have expected the news I shocked her with when she came back from Florida.

"I'm up here, c'mon up!" Trish shouted.

When I stepped into the spare bedroom Trish had made into her office, I found her sitting at a brand-new desk/wall unit combination.

"Wow, nice! Where did you find this?"

"Online. It came in multiple boxes and took all week to assemble," Trish said.

"Really? You put this monster together by yourself? I know you're good at following assembly instructions, but this is massive. I am impressed."

Like me, Trish kept busy when upset. I always respected her independence and ability to complete large projects, but this was a complex assembly. Seeing this reinforced my confidence in her capacity to deal with our upcoming challenges.

"Thanks. Welcome home, honey."

I bent over and gave her a kiss, then sat next to her. "What's new?" I asked, hoping we would get to the matter immediately.

"I want to hear about your trip, but not before I tell you what I've decided while you were away," Trish replied.

"Yeah, go ahead, I'm anxious to hear it."

I was way past anxious; I was still deeply concerned.

Trish leaned back in her chair and swiveled it towards me.

"The first days you were gone, I struggled with everything. I didn't have any idea how we could survive as a couple. Where do I fit into this new life of yours? Are we going to feel safe wherever we go, or are we going to live in constant fear?"

"Those are important concerns, Trish, and I can't honestly say I have answers yet, but…"

Trish interrupted me mid-sentence. I was startled; she never did that.

"Let me finish what I have to say before you comment, please," she said.

"No problem, go ahead."

"I did lots of research while you were gone. I found an essay online written by a woman whose husband of many years decided he couldn't go on living as a man anymore and needed to become a woman. The similarities were striking and hit me hard."

The sudden shift in the conversation's tone made me suspicious.

Where was she going with this? Did this unknown woman leave her husband? Was she influencing Trish's decision to remain with me? What did she mean by "hit me hard"?

"That's interesting. What's the essay titled?"

"Goodbye Husband, Hello Wife," Trish replied.

Goodbye husband? I didn't like the way that began, but hello, wife... that could mean acceptance.

"I want to share something." Trish slid her chair over to her keyboard and opened her emails. As she began to read, it dawned on me that she had written to the woman who authored the article. I listened as she shared my experience—our experience—with this stranger. Tears welled up in my eyes as she detailed her agony and concerns through this letter. I knew revealing my truth was going to be difficult for Trish, but this was a stark reminder of how difficult it was, and how alone she must have felt while I was on my trip.

I pictured her alone at her desk, I far away in Florida, surrounded by support onstage at the club. I was celebrating my newfound freedom while she was sending emails out into space, waiting for a reply.

"It makes me sad to think of you reaching out to strangers just so you can feel like you're not alone," I said.

"Well, she's not really a stranger."

"What do you mean?"

"She wrote back to me, and she's been incredibly supportive and helpful."

I felt my breathing quicken. Was this unknown person actually advising Trish?

"She told me that part of her journey was realizing their love went beyond physical gender and lived in their hearts."

I began to feel relief.

"I'm impressed you found such an insightful connection, Trish. It gives me hope, too. I'm amazed by the initiative you've taken."

Relief was understating how I felt. Moments before, I had been deeply concerned that this was a breaking point. Suddenly, it turned for the better.

"Thanks. Knowing a couple in a comparable situation has stayed together and is making it work is evidence that we can do this," Trish replied.

We can do this! Did I hear that correctly? My hopes were reinforced.

"I remember Doctor Deb saying that when you transition, everyone you love transitions with you. It's going to be a hard road, but if I have you with me, I know we can make it," I said.

Trish took my hand.

"That's good. Because I decided I wouldn't let you go through this alone."

This is Trish's email, which she shared with me:

I have just re-read your article. I have lost count of how many times I have read it. In January, my husband of 30 years told me he was transgender and had started seeing a therapist. I had known he liked to dress. On Halloween, we would go on vacation to the gay district in Ft Lauderdale, where he could go in "costume." I did not know the extent of his feelings.

He has known he has felt like a girl since he was 4 years old. He is now 63. At this time, he will not go through the physical transition. We have discussed this, but his business would be lost if this were known, and some of his family would not understand. I want to give him support. I am trying, but my feelings are confusing. I will go to his next therapy session with him, and I'm going to have his therapist read your article. It puts into words my feelings.

I am not sure why I'm writing to you. I think I just wanted to thank you for sharing your story. It gives me some comfort.

Trisha T.

A few days went by, and we awkwardly settled into our chairs at Doctor Deb's office. We were both on edge, anxious to establish a road map to guide us through this untraveled territory we found ourselves in. I began by informing Doctor Deb of Trish's communication with the author and the resulting decision to explore our possibilities together.

"Wow, Trish! I'm so happy to see you're both on board with this," Dr. Deb exclaimed.

Doctor Deb looked my way. "You must have been relieved to hear about it."

"Relieved and ecstatic," I replied.

"Have you decided to begin transitioning now?" Doctor Deb said.

"Yes and no," I replied. "We're looking for a starting point. I'm willing to slowly phase out of my business as I transition. I think I can cut back on appearances and work with customers online entirely as we get deeper into making physical changes."

Trish added, "We've agreed transition has to begin now, but carefully and gradually. Are there things we can do to get started that aren't noticeable to others?"

Doctor Deb rubbed the back of her neck, perhaps relieving the tension.

"Not very much. You can't even do the smallest of things before getting a second opinion from a licensed therapist, which is required before you can see any doctors or surgeons. As a matter of fact, I can't sign your 'Medically Necessary' sworn statement until you've gotten confirmation from another gender therapist. I can recommend someone if you'd like."

"Yes, that sounds reasonable."

"Are these WPATH guidelines?" Trish asked.

"Yes, very good, Trish!" Doctor Deb exclaimed. "Everything I'll explain in this process is."

"What then?" I asked.

"The next step is to refer you to a medical doctor who will review this information, examine you, and then get you started on hormone replacement therapy," Doctor Deb replied.

"Will there be visible effects from the hormones?" I asked.

"Very minor in the first year. You may develop small breasts. Your skin will soften."

"Small breasts? Will they be noticeable?" Trish asked.

"Barely, but easily concealed," Doctor Deb replied.

"What else can I do in advance of surgery?" I asked.

"You might consider starting facial hair removal as soon as possible. Electrolysis is a long, arduous process. It can take hundreds of hours. I would recommend starting hormones as soon as you decide to begin. Doctors will need proof that you have been on them for at least one year prior to any surgeries."

I did the math in my head, realizing that the extra year would be added to the time spent in a semi-transitional state, doing only a few minor things. It could be two or three years before I finally became the complete woman I wanted to be. There was no time to waste. I wanted to begin immediately, but still faced the same problems.

"I understand those are the guidelines, but another year… haven't I waited long enough? Aren't there exceptions for time served in this male body? I'm not sure I can wait that extra year once we decide to go all in."

"Then let's get you that appointment for the second opinion. The sooner you do that, the sooner these small steps can be taken. I think you would be wise to start as soon as possible. That will start the clock on the year you have to wait."

"I'm all for anything we can do to speed up the timetable," I said.

"Yes, time is not our friend here. It's the downside of transitioning later in life. Try to remember what you've been through in your lifetime. Isn't it a miracle that you now have the opportunity to actually make this happen? You've been there for everyone else over the years, and now it's your turn."

"I have to keep reminding myself how wonderful it is. I never believed I would reach a point in my life where this was within reach, but I want it now," I said.

We left her office with mixed emotions. We were positioned at the starting gate, but still had to formulate an exit strategy for the business.

"How did you think that went?" Trish asked.

"I'm ready to just scream *fuck the business*, but I can't quite do that yet," I replied.

"You'll find a way. We haven't come this far for nothing. Just hang in there, it'll happen."

Chapter Twenty-Four:
The End of The Beginning

Trish and I decided to tell one person in my family to test the waters. The plan was to follow that up with an email to the rest of the family and some close friends, detailing my lifelong struggle and my recent diagnosis. I would reveal everything, except the frustration of spinning my wheels in the muddy sludge of any attempt to accelerate my transition.

I chose to start with my sister Joanne. I loved and trusted every one of my siblings, but this was the logical place for me to start. Trish and I had lived near her for many years in Minnesota and spent several Easter Sundays with Joanne and her husband, Don. We also traditionally had a Christmas gingerbread house building party at their home, laughing at each other's houses as the walls collapsed or roofs fell in from too much candy decoration and poor structural support.

It was early spring, and we thought it best to wait a few weeks, drive to Minnesota, then begin the task by telling them. They were both teachers and very compassionate people. I was sure this was the place to start. The week before Easter Sunday, I received a call from my brother-in-law, Don.

He informed me that Joanne had been experiencing severe heart problems and was on life-saving medication. What was saving her heart had caused severe damage to her kidneys. This condition had advanced to the point where a decision had to be made. She could risk dialysis or give up the heart medication. Neither was a good option. Whichever treatment was selected was going to affect the other negatively. She quickly entered hospice care. Shocked and without a clue as to whether she had days, weeks, or months to live, we left early Thursday morning for the drive to Minneapolis from Chicago.

"This reminds me of what happened to Jerry," I said to Trish.

A few years earlier, my brother in Texas had suffered a massive stroke and entered a care facility. He had always been a gregarious person who never struggled to find words, and it was extremely difficult to see him in a condition that left him unable to speak without struggle. His frustration was evident and heartbreaking.

When I visited him in the care facility, I recalled how he took me in when I moved to Texas and helped me find a career path. I was naïve to the ways of the business world, and he had been my mentor. A few weeks later, he died in that facility. I was devastated. He was the first of my siblings to pass away.

"Remember what Joanne said to me after I spoke at Jerry's service? It's so ironic now," I said.

"What was that?" Trish asked.

"'Your eulogy was so good. I want you to do mine!'" I replied.

"What did you say to her?"

"I told her I'd be happy to, then I said wait, that didn't come out right, and we both laughed."

"You guys were just trying to lighten things up."

"How quickly things change," I said.

Joanne was sleeping when we arrived at the sprawling 1970s rambler-style hospice facility. As I stood by her bedside with Trish, she opened her eyes, looked at us for a moment, then said, "You two are so cute!"

I smiled at that and held her hand. I was always uncomfortable in these situations and struggled to find words.

"I love you, Joannie, and I just wanted you to know how sorry I am for being such a little asshole when you guys brought me into your home after Mom and Dad died," I said.

I had no idea why that came out of my mouth. I had apologized several years ago, and there were no unresolved issues.

"Oh no, no, you were so young, and we were all grieving. That's long forgotten," she replied.

My throat tightened, and I choked back the tears. "I guess I just don't know what to say."

"That's a first," she said softly, with a smile.

"Hah! Yeah, I don't usually have that problem. I just love you so much, I…"

"I know that, and you don't need to tell me what I already know," she said, tightening her grip on my hand.

She was fading back into sleep, so we thought we should let her rest.

"We'll be just outside. I'm sure we'll talk later," I told her.

Trish and I left her side with teary eyes and heavy hearts. Our brief talk was overshadowed by the truth. We didn't know if this was our last conversation.

By the time Saturday came, we were emotionally spent. It had been a very long couple of days. Watching loved ones coming in and out of her room, upset and crying, became increasingly difficult. We retreated to the back of the house, a small room with four chairs that had a serene view of the backyard trees. We held hands as I released the tears I'd been restraining.

"I know how difficult this is for you," Trish said.

"It's not easy for either of us. Too much emotional turmoil in me right now. I don't know how much longer I can keep my news a secret. I feel like I'll explode if I don't tell someone, but I can't do that to any of my brothers or sisters at a time like this."

"Maybe you need to tell someone else. Can you think of whom you can confide in and trust?"

"I've been thinking about that, and I keep coming back to our niece Gina. She has her PhD in psychology and is a progressive-minded person. She also has a good understanding of the human condition."

"She'd be the perfect one to talk to, but don't you think Mary Jane would be hurt that you told her daughter, not her?"

"No. I think under the circumstances, she'll understand why I didn't speak to any of my brothers or sisters first."

The opportunity to tell Gina arose quickly. Trish had gone to grab a soda, and I had just poured myself yet another cup of coffee when Gina walked into the room.

"Are you OK, Uncle Mike?" she said.

"As good as any of us are right now. And you?"

"It's tough. Joanne has been like a second mom to me. I've always had a strong bond with her."

"Yeah, I knew that you two had been close. You're a thoughtful, caring person, just like her and your mom."

I hesitated for a long moment, unsure if this was the right time or place. I squirmed in my chair, then decided it was now or never.

"I have something I need to talk about, and I think you are the one I can confide in. It's deeply personal, and I trust you. I was going to tell Joanne before this happened, but now I believe you can help me out."

She looked startled. Her eyes focused intensely on mine.

"You can talk to me! I appreciate your trust. I would be willing to hear whatever it is you have on your mind, and I'll keep it to myself. Whatever it is you are going through, I'll do my best to help," Gina said.

"That's great, give me a few minutes to find Trish. I think she should be with us. This involves her as well."

"Are you guys having problems?"

"It's not what you think, not in a million years. Why don't the three of us take a walk in the park across the street? It's quiet and peaceful."

Trish was sitting in the common living area, across from visitors from another family. I sat next to her and quietly said, "We should go for a walk across the street. Gina is going to join us."

Trish knew what I meant, but couldn't believe it happened so soon. "Really, already? We only discussed this half an hour ago. She's ok with it?"

"I didn't reveal anything. I wanted you to be there, but yes, she really wants to help."

I helped Trish out of her chair, and we headed outside.

The three of us made small talk as we walked into the park. I stepped ahead, next to Gina, and began to reveal my life and therapy breakthrough.

"Oh my God, I had no idea, but I am relieved. I was sure you were going to tell me you were dying or something!" Gina said.

"No, no, I'm just realizing what I need to do to live fully," I replied.

She gave me a huge hug, then we continued to walk as Trish trailed behind us. We walked and talked for an hour or so. I did most of the talking, and Trish made a few comments, but mostly listened.

I was incredibly relieved to have informed someone in my family. Time had passed so quickly that I didn't remember most of the conversation. It was a whirlwind of revelation and emotional relief.

Gina was incredibly supportive, and I knew I had made the right decision concerning who I should tell. We agreed to keep the dialogue going, and she would help me as much as she could.

When you run a one-person business, there's no one to fill in while you're away. There were things I absolutely had to get home to take care of for customers first thing Monday. We waited until early afternoon Easter Sunday, and when there was no change in Joanne's condition, we made the hard choice to drive home.

"Do you want to talk about whatever it is that's bothering you?" I said after we'd driven over a hundred miles in complete silence. Trish was avoiding eye contact and gazing out her side window. I sensed her aggravation.

"You are obviously pissed off at me," I said.

Trish's body language shifted her away from me, closer to her door. She remained silent.

"You want to share what's on your mind?" I asked.

"Oh, now you care about my feelings and what I think. A little late, isn't it?" Trish replied.

"What are you talking about? When have I not cared?" I said.

"You really don't know, do you?" Trish said incredulously.

Now, I was upset.

"You know, we could try one of those guessing games people play with their kids to occupy the time on a car trip, but I would prefer you just tell me what the hell you're talking about."

"Sure, sarcasm! That always puts me in the mood to talk."

"Then just tell me, please!" I said.

"You don't realize how much it hurts me to listen to you go on and on about yourself with Gina about this MOMENTOUS breakthrough. Finding your long-lost self and the ecstasy of becoming who you are. All of that is great, but you didn't even mention my feelings to her or go out of your way to include me in the conversation."

Trish took me by surprise. I had to refocus on the road. I didn't see it quite the way she did.

"That is just not true. I'm not that selfish. Sure, I went on about myself, but Gina was the first family member I told, and it just poured out of me. I thought you understood why I was so unrelenting in my revelation. I let it all out in the open at once, and it was spontaneous."

"You made me feel like I wasn't even a part of this, as if it didn't affect me."

I had been concerned about Trish all along and worried about her well-being every minute of the day. I didn't think she was being fair towards me.

"I don't think you're listening to me. I just explained that my emotions were in the stratosphere, my mouth got ahead of my brain, and I'm overwhelmed with the fact that my sister is probably dying."

Trish crossed her arms, leaned away from me, and went back into silent mode. I waited a few uncomfortably long minutes for her to respond.

"Nothing to say about that? No 'apology accepted'? I have to tell you, Trish, if this is how it's going to be every time I share my story or explain the complications, then maybe we should just forget the whole thing."

"Oh, that's really mature. Stop being a big baby."

"Right. Then your silent movie starlet act isn't at all childish?"

I began doubting whether I should go through ANY transitioning now. Would our lives be this complicated? Even more so once I began? The strain on our relationship could get much worse than this, the further into the process we went. It was all so vague and unclear. My mind was going in a direction I hadn't prepared for as the silent miles passed.

Still in Wisconsin, only a few hours from home, we needed to stop for gas.

"You want something to eat? We haven't eaten since this morning," I said.

"Yeah, I guess so," Trish replied.

I pulled into a fast-food drive-through, and we ate in the car without saying much.

Just as we finished, my phone rang. It was Gina. I put her on speakerphone.

"Hey, you guys, I'm sorry to have to break this to you, Joanne passed away this evening."

We were silent for a moment, then I replied. "We really didn't expect this to happen so soon, Gina. I don't have any words right now, except to say we love you, and thank you for letting us know."

"Yes, I'm speechless too. I love you both. Have a safe trip home."

I placed both hands on the steering wheel, slumped forward, and wept. Trish was crying as she put her hand on my shoulder, gently massaging my neck.

"I'm so sorry, honey, I know how much you love her. I love her too; this is so sad."

"Thank you. We knew this was coming, but the finality of it is hard to accept," I replied.

We said a quiet prayer for her, gathered our composure, and got back on the highway home.

"Trish," I said a few minutes later, "I'm sorry that I became overly excited for myself when I unburdened everything to Gina. I honestly got caught up in the moment and never intended to hurt you."

"I know that. I understand why you got carried away. You were happy, and you were running on pure adrenaline. You've always been considerate of my feelings and tried to include me. I'm sorry I got mad too," Trish said.

"I just can't believe how quickly this all developed. Less than a week ago, we were planning a visit to tell her everything... and suddenly, she's gone."

"Life really is too short, honey. You need to begin a complete transition. You've waited long enough. You need to get approval for hormones as soon as we get home so we can take the next steps," Trish said, out of the blue.

"I was thinking the same, but no half-measures. I need to complete all the preliminary requirements, interview doctors, and schedule surgeries. In the meantime, I can also begin electrolysis."

"I agree. It's time. You've always put business first, but you know what? FUCK the business!" Trish said.

I was shocked Trish said that, but it made me feel better.

"Absolutely *fuck* the business. I'm done worrying about it. I can't keep going with the 'do a few things, see where the business is, do a few more things, reassess' attitude. It's just too damn hopeless."

"I don't care about the money; this is the important thing right now. Your well-being and happiness are intertwined with mine. We can't go on worrying about everyone else's opinion," Trish said.

"Thanks for saying that. I'm sick of putting on this male clown suit every day to entertain everyone's perception of right and wrong. I've played that game far too long, and to hell with anyone who judges me for who I really am," I replied.

"And we are going to be judged and hated. We will lose friends," Trish said.

"Exactly, but the friends we lose would not be a loss. Our real friends, the ones who know our hearts, will support us entirely."

"True, but what about Florida? What do we do there? We have lots of friends, but I'm worried about our safety beyond the gates of our community," Trish said.

"Culturally speaking, not a great environment for trans people. We will just have to play it day to day and figure it out."

"Wow. This escalated quickly. It sounds like we've both been doing a lot of thinking," Trish said.

"No doubt. I think we know which path to take and when to take it."

We quietly absorbed everything we'd just said, then I spoke.

"We were going to talk to Joanne, but I'm pretty sure she's been doing all the talking in the last half hour."

"That's a beautiful thought, honey. I think you're right. Her courage in the end has inspired our new beginning," Trish said.

"There will be so much uncertainty ahead, so many trapdoors and risks. We will need that inspiration. Doctor Deb warned that this would be like jumping off a cliff, you don't know who will be with you, or what's waiting at the bottom."

Trish thought about that for a minute, grasped my hand, and said, "We'll jump together then."

Clarity came to me in that moment; there were no doubts. It was time to go all-in.

"For as long as I can remember, I have been desperate to find a place in this world where I can completely become a woman, and now, it's right in front of me. It's time to step up and take it."

"I love you more now than ever," Trish said.

"And I love you with all of my heart and soul. I could not do this without you," I replied.

"You WILL do it, and I'll be with you every step of the way."

Chapter Twenty-Five: Epilogue

When I finally began transitioning, I was in my sixties. The physical and mental strain was magnified by my advancing age. Recovery and healing took longer, and I constantly battled emotional fatigue.

Following two major surgeries, I completed hundreds of hours of electrolysis over the weekends at a clinic in the far northern suburbs of Chicago. I would do 12-hour sessions with two electrologists simultaneously working on each side of my face, resulting in a swollen face that looked like raw hamburger.

I'd spend the remainder of the weekend recovering in a hotel room nearby. The facial redness and scabbing were severe to the point of appearing freakish and grotesque. I would have to stay in my room until the swelling subsided, then go home late Sunday night. The burning sensation didn't subside for several days. Over the following 16 months, I'd repeat the process every two weeks.

Back at the hotel, Trish would usually say something like, "Oh my God! That looks horrible. You must want this desperately to go through so much pain and discomfort. You look like a tortured blowfish!"

"No, I just woke up one day on a whim and decided I wanted to be a woman," I replied.

We would both laugh. She knew I was referring to remarks made by anti-trans comedians and conservative talk show hosts who claimed this was a fad and not a 'real condition.' But then, we'd lived the truth. We understood what I had been through and what it took for me to reach this point. Their comments were ignorant and served the purpose of strengthening my pain tolerance while igniting my resolve. Those close to me, who saw what I was going through, would ask, "Why did you wait until it was so late in your life to do this?" or "Is it worth all of the physical pain and social risk?"

It wasn't that I wanted to wait. I could not find a path to revealing the truth until I fully realized exactly what the truth was. The longer I was in denial, the harder it became to reach that conclusion.

The more personal and business relationships I developed, the greater the risk of losing. Both denial and acceptance became more perilous as time went on. It truly was a double-edged sword. I felt like I was letting myself down whichever direction I chose.

It took a lot of courage for me to face the truth and reach out for professional help. I found that inspiration to face mine in part because of the high-profile trans people who came out very publicly.

Their doing so resulted in mass media attention to our plight. Now that celebrities were involved, the media began taking gender dysphoria seriously.

Katie Couric did a comprehensive documentary titled *Gender Revolution* for the National Geographic Channel, featuring expert testimony from physicians and scientists, including evidence supporting the realities of gender dysphoria. Her interviews with trans people of all ages and identities shed light on their struggles for rights and acceptance, as well as the joy of finally becoming whole.

She also interviewed parents, siblings, and friends of trans people who loved and accepted the person dealing with being transgender. It was profoundly touching and resonated in my heart.

A significant effort was being made to understand what transgender people have been going through. The presentations were well-produced and compassionate. Were we no longer just a punchline to a bad joke? Could this sudden positive attention minimize the public's attitude of fear and mistrust?

I began asking myself, "Why not me? When is it my turn?" If others can become themselves this publicly, why can't I? I wasn't naïve enough to believe that everyone felt this way, but the world was changing enough for me to change as well. So I thought at the time.

When I healed from the surgeries to the point that I was able to dress presentably and go out in public, it was like the entire world had changed before my eyes. I felt the way one does after getting a pair of glasses for the first time; I'd succeeded in aligning my outside with my inside, and the world around me leapt into sharp focus. All of the pain simply fell away. The joy was beyond anything I have ever experienced. For the first time in my life, I was completely myself. No hiding, no guilt, no pretending to be male. I was thrilled to be who I always knew I was, but never imagined I could be.

However, it took time to adjust. I often found myself assuming everyone was looking at me and projecting that they were judging me. I was self-aware enough to catch it and realize I didn't have any idea what people were thinking; I was projecting my fears, as I had done when I went out on my own for the first time in Fort Lauderdale. Certainly, there were times I could tell people were actually giving me nasty looks or making comments, but for the most part, people were very kind.

But the peak of my initial newfound happiness came in a tender moment, in a fashionable ladies' shop in downtown Naperville, Illinois. Trish and I had shopped there many times before my surgeries. The ladies working there always treated me kindly and respectfully. The first time I returned after healing, fully dressed and made up, I received so much love, hugs, and positive vibes, I could hardly stand it. They set aside a dressing room for me to try on the outfits we picked out. They put my name on the door in big letters, 'BELLA.' I was overwhelmed to the point of tears.

"You know you guys have a customer for life now, right?" This boosted my confidence and alleviated my fear of using ladies' fitting rooms.

Trish was instrumental in building my confidence as well. Initially, I was insecure about applying my makeup. Was it too much, not enough, or did it look natural? Trish would be honest and let me know if it did not look good.

At times, I thought she was being too critical, and I pushed back. "Isn't it ever good enough?" She would just scoff and say, "You're going through the teenage girl thing, I'm trying to help, I'm not the bad mom here."

When it became apparent that I was getting better at it, she was encouraging, yet funny.

"How do I look today? Is this good?" I said.

"Beautiful," she replied. "You look absolutely beautiful." Then, after a dramatic pause, she'd say, "BITCH!" We laughed then—and still joke about it today.

We adjusted well to life in the Chicago area, but it became difficult for us to maintain two homes in different states. We still had the townhome in Illinois and the condo in Florida. We had to settle in one location as we looked forward to retirement.

We decided to sell both places and buy a single-family home in Florida. We purchased a home in a beautiful community. We made friends quickly and felt safe amidst the love and support of our newfound neighbors. We became part of a loving church community where our involvement was enthusiastically welcomed. We were certain we would never have to move again, and this would be our "happily ever after home."

But within a few quick years, the sweetness began to sour, and our happiness faded.

A couple of incidents spurred outrage among Republican leaders in various states, one of them being Florida. The facts were manipulated, and fear was spread through a wave of political misinformation. Trans people were being accused of entering women's restrooms for the sole purpose of invading privacy and possibly assaulting cisgender women, yet there had been no evidence of that.

A teenage boy, not transgender, put on a skirt and entered a girls' restroom at a school in Virginia, and was accused of assaulting a girl. This resulted in panic and protests against the trans community nationally and spawned bathroom restriction laws.

History was repeating itself in the ugliest way. Whenever a small minority makes inroads towards acceptance and normalization, panic and lies are spread in an attempt to squash progress.

Republican politicians focused their attacks on the transgender population to gain favor among conservative voters. They used lies to create a bogeyman, and in a cowardly move, held children out in front of themselves as human shields. "They're coming for your kids!" This was the battle cry of the self-appointed culture warriors.

Marco Rubio, a United States Senator from Florida, ran a campaign ad against his opponent in his 2022 re-election bid in which he claimed, "My opponent supports liberal teachers who want to turn our boys into girls!" Those were his exact words, and if he believes it is possible, or that this was what being transgender is about, he should not hold a position of responsibility anywhere! Yet in Florida, he won re-election.

The bigots presented themselves as champions of your children, claiming to protect them from a conspiracy of indoctrination that does not exist, a theme all too familiar among the gay community in their struggles for acceptance.

Before the vote on the bill titled 'Safety in Public Spaces,' aimed at barring transgender adults from using restrooms or locker rooms other than those matching their "assigned gender at birth," Florida Statehouse Rep. Webster Barnaby addressed the chamber and protested trans people: "I'm watching this like an X-Men movie. It's like mutants living among us — not of this world, not of my God. They are demons and imps pretending to be human. Vote yes on this bill!"

No representative objected. The bill passed.

Over time, this relentlessly anti-trans political agenda made Trish and me feel unsafe in our chosen home. In public places, I was suddenly disrespected and treated as though I were less than. In the ladies' clothing section of a major department store, I selected a few items to try on. I was having trouble finding a fitting room, and asked a store clerk where one was available. She looked directly at me, rolled her eyes, and said, "I don't think we have one for you, sir!"

I was shocked by her rudeness and deliberate misgendering. I remained calm. I worried she would call security and make up a wild story, accusing me of causing fear among female customers.

I laid the clothes on her check-out counter and said, "That's OK, I don't need to spend my money where customers are treated this poorly."

I thought of reporting her to the store manager, but in this blazing hot political climate, how could I be sure they wouldn't call the police? Driving home, it occurred to me that I wasn't sure what the local police were capable of doing to me if I were to be stopped and questioned for anything!

I began to fear driving anywhere. I no longer trusted Florida police to respect my rights.

The smallest misstep could lead to a "resisting arrest" or "creating a public disturbance" charge. I could be arrested for no reason or even beaten, for all I knew. When the governing body of the state I lived in passed laws against me with great prejudice, who would protect my rights?

The police, or a local judge? I couldn't count on that. My thoughts drifted back to my arrest as a teenager. Going back those many years, I knew I never wanted any kind of trouble with the law again.

My fears were palpable and ever-present. I could not rely on equal protection under the law.

When you are a six-foot, one-inch-tall transwoman, you're not inconspicuous. It's impossible to be stealthy. I felt like a target wherever I went. I had another experience at the local supermarket: "Find everything you needed today, sir?" the young man at the check-out register said sarcastically. I wanted to pull up my top and flash my breasts, but I ignored the insult and said, "Yeah, I did, thank you."

"Come back soon, SIR," he replied.

Once was enough. He was pushing my buttons now.

"No, I don't think I will…. BOY!" I shot back.

He was surprised and turned red. Immature young white men in Florida hate being called "boy."

I walked away as he muttered something under his breath. This deliberate misgendering continued in other transactional situations. The hardware store, drug store, restaurants, coffee shops, and many other places where I previously felt safe no longer treated me kindly. People who had been quietly prejudiced against trans people were now emboldened and encouraged by politicians and conservative talk show hosts who gave them the green light to hate. It was as though the dormant body snatchers had been awakened and released from their pods.

If laws were required to restrain trans people on a choke collar, it would be ok to treat them like animals, right? I tried to stop picturing worst-case scenarios, but I couldn't help thinking that Trish and I needed to get out of Florida before things got worse.

Minnesota was starting to seem better and better to us. The Governor of Minnesota had just passed new laws protecting transgender rights, in direct contradiction of the new Florida laws, declaring Minnesota a sanctuary state for transpeople.

Meanwhile, Governor Ron DeSantis announced his measures to ensure the safety of Florida children by making it criminal for parents to get treatment for their transgender children. He somehow knew what was best for everyone else's children. They could be arrested and charged with a crime for any attempt to help their own child who is suffering from gender dysphoria. Also, doctors who issued hormone therapy or any type of treatment to under-18 transgendered patients would have broken the law, would be arrested, and would face prison sentences.

Adding insult to injury, he publicly declared, "Transgender is not a real condition. In time, these children will grow out of this phase and get over it."

This is the most demeaning thing you can say about trans people: that we are frauds, fakes, not real, we just need to grow up. Laws were also passed to make it difficult for transgender adults to obtain hormone therapy and other necessary treatments.

The Uninvited Passenger

Trish and I were watching the local news when those restrictions were announced. I'd reached the end of my rope and ranted on.

"Transpeople can't do this and can't do that, and we've done so many awful things that the country is being overrun by us! Oh my God! You would think there were millions of us, ruthlessly descending upon society like the zombie apocalypse! We are not even one-tenth of a percent of the population. How could we possibly be everywhere, doing all of these horrible things all at the same time?"

Trish responded quietly. "I don't feel good about being in Florida anymore," she said.

"Neither do I. I don't feel comfortable or safe."

"I'm worried about someone hurting you, Bella."

"I'm worried about you, too, about both of us, Trish."

"We can't keep living like this. What are we going to do?" Trish replied.

"It's late. Let's sleep on it and talk tomorrow," I said.

Neither of us slept much that night. The next morning, we walked into the kitchen, pulled up our chairs, and sat quietly.

"I've been thinking all night, and I know what we need to do," Trish announced.

"Please, tell me what that is!" I replied.

"You're going to think this sounds crazy," Trish said.

I didn't have a clue where she was headed. I got out of my chair and stood behind hers.

"Do I look like someone who cares if something sounds crazy?" I asked.

Turning her head to face me, Trish replied,

"We need to sell this house and go back to Minnesota."

I was stunned. I never imagined she would even think about going back home. I didn't have to think for one second about my response.

"I am so relieved! I can't believe you said that. I have been thinking the same, but didn't want to suggest moving. I know how much you love our home and friends here, and so do I, but it really is the smart choice now," I replied.

"Minnesota is a better place for us. We have more family, lots of friends, and the transgender acceptance level is very strong," Trish said.

"Right, and given the recent changes Governor Walz enacted in Minnesota, it's even stronger. Lots of parents are already moving with their children, so they can get the care they need without the prospect of being jailed," I replied.

We put the house on the market a few days later. It sold within a week. With all the regrets of leaving behind friends, the church congregation, and our home, Trish and I returned to Minnesota.

"I'm getting too old for this crap," I said as I dropped a heavy box marked "cookware" on the kitchen floor of our new home.

"Promise me we are *never* moving again," Trish replied. "We're both too old for this crap!"

I got down on the floor to straighten up the box I'd dropped.

"You have my word, n*ever* again. My body cannot take this kind of punishment. Besides, I'm pretty sure I've developed a cardboard and tape allergy," I replied.

Trish bent over to help with the box.

"But really, you must be as thrilled as I am to be back here?" she said.

I didn't hesitate.

"Are you kidding me? I can't remember when I've felt so good to be anywhere! The difference between how I'm treated here as opposed to Florida is phenomenal."

Trish knew what I meant, but loved hearing me say I was finally happy.

"So what makes you so happy to be here?" she asked.

I got up off the floor, dusted off, and took a seat in our new breakfast nook.

"You've been with me and seen how respectful most people are here. They go out of their way to call me 'ma'am' or say, 'Have a nice day, ladies.' I'm at the highest level of acceptance and comfort I've felt since transitioning."

Trish put her arm on my shoulder as she stood behind me.

"I'm happy to hear that, because I'm overjoyed to be back home. I didn't realize how much I missed it here."

I had noticed how enthusiastic, relieved, and happy she'd been since we came back.

"We will miss our friends in Florida, though," I said.

"That's for sure, but maybe if things change for the better down there, we can go visit."

"Maybe, but I wouldn't count on that anytime soon. Cultural changes don't happen overnight. We'll just continue to be grateful that we're home, and for now, that's good enough for me."

When I decided to write this book, my goal was to give people a better understanding of what being transgender is like over the course of a lifetime: not in a glimpse, or a sound byte, but a vivid understanding informed by empathizing with one person's convictions and accomplishments.

I hoped that if readers got to know me, their understanding of trans people in general would broaden and deepen. We do not have a large voice because we are an extremely small minority. I would like people to find familiarity in our common human traits of love, loss, humor, compassion, and most of all, hope.

I was more hopeful when I began writing, but politicians have been very busy hijacking progress to give themselves credibility among others who think like them. Despite the success they have claimed, I still hang onto hope. Even as they continue to make the world fear transgender people, I have found comfort within myself as never before. I have discovered solace in my journey that cannot be taken away.

I also hoped to help young trans people understand themselves better. I want to encourage them to take their time, think things through, and get professional help. You will know in time what is best. This is far too serious and life-changing to act abruptly. Most of all, hang onto your dignity, self-respect, and promises of a bright future.

Did I wait too long to transition? Probably, but if I'd made different choices, I wouldn't have met Trish or had the specific experiences that make me the person I am today.

In spite of the fact that I dealt with so much despair in my own youth, I never gave up on hope for a better life. Eventually, I found a love worth waiting for, and a life worth living. Trish and I are proof that it is wise to be patient, hold out for your best life, and never underestimate the resiliency of the human spirit.

Acknowledgements and Thanks

Doctor Deborah Wilke
For digging up everything I had buried over a lifetime, shaking off the dust, and guiding me through the process of making sense of it all. I would not have found my true self without your expertise and compassion. You are a treasured gift to the Transgender community.

Sarah Terez Rosenblum
My writing mentor, guide, teacher, and encouraging force. Your skilled instruction took me from a raw talent to someone who could share her story with the world in an interesting, compelling way. Thank you for being a great friend and ally.

Heather N. Wilde with Hezzie Mae Publishing
Thank you for being the megaphone, giving volume to the voices of independent writers and authentic, personal stories to share with the world. Your advocacy and passion for those marginalized are crucial.

My family and friends
Your acceptance, love, and support have been, and always will be, the most important part of my journey.

Author Bio

Isabella (Bella) Tousignant is an independent writer, speaker, and entrepreneur, living authentically as herself without remorse.

She began transitioning at the age of 63 and has a unique perspective on the myths, challenges, and truth surrounding gender dysphoria.

A strong proponent of transgender rights, her goal is to engage in open discussion, honesty, familiarity, and acceptance, which begins with this book.

At a time when truth is obscured for political gain, and 'scorched earth' mandates are removing civil rights, Bella's well-documented lived experience brings those truths into the light.

CONNECT WITH THE AUTHOR

Email: isabellatous@gmail.com

LEAVE A REVIEW

If you enjoyed reading *The Uninvited Passenger*, would you consider leaving a review on the platform of your choice? Reviews help indie-published authors find more readers like you.

www.ingramcontent.com/pod-product-compliance
Lightning Source LLC
Chambersburg PA
W070613030426
37CB00020B/3784